WRITING GOOD SENTENCES

A Friendly Manual

Mildred M. Jeffrey
Associate Professor of English Emerita, Hofstra University

authorHOUSE®

AuthorHouse™
1663 Liberty Drive
Bloomington, IN 47403
www.authorhouse.com
Phone: 1-800-839-8640

Published by AuthorHouse   01/08/2013

ISBN: 978-1-4772-9220-4 (sc)
ISBN: 978-1-4772-9219-8 (e)

Library of Congress Control Number: 2012921957

This book is printed on acid-free paper.

ALSO BY MILDRED M. JEFFREY

Fiction
Daughter, Oh My Daughter
(to be reprinted as The Downtown Train)
Walking The Cliffs
Rejoice
Two Against A Kingdom

Poetry
Detours and Intersections
Dear Mr. Wordsworth
True Lies

To Chuck
who makes good things happen

FOREWORD

A grammar can never have the precision of a mathematics text. Any description of language is bound to reflect the disparities and inconsistencies of its human users. Therefore it is wise for the student of language to abandon a search for explanation when faced with the exception to a rule.

OVERVIEW

Learning a language means gaining control over its three aspects—vocabulary, sentence construction, and correct usage. Vocabulary is the most important aspect of language, both for speaking and writing. Sentence construction is essential for writing. Correct usage, both in speaking and writing, is of least importance for a number of reasons.

First, even without respecting correct usage, you can often make yourself understood. ("I ain't got no money" might horrify your teacher, but it conveys its meaning vividly.) Second, correct usage changes. For instance, many out-of-date textbooks still preach the use of "whom" (as in "Whom do you wish to see?" although no one but an old-fashioned school marm would say anything other than "Who do you wish to see?"). It is wise to check the copyright date of your manual of correct usage if you are relying on one. Third, some points of correct usage are open to debate in the real world even though a dated textbook might still be arbitrary. (See note later on under "infinitives.") Fourth, correct usage varies according to the level of language use your reader or audience expects—formal, colloquial (everyday), slangy, or hip hop. For example, the politician who speaks with fastidious attention to the old-fashioned niceties of English will lose the support of people like Joe Six-pack, who wants to vote for "a regular guy." A majority of Americans scorn anything that suggests elitism.

This book will focus on the second aspect of language—sentence construction for written English. Contemporary use of English in e-mail, blogs, and text-messaging does not fall within the scope of this book, nor does spoken English, which does not rely on the sentence. Most of the interchange of daily conversations consists of sentence fragments and single words sometimes even overlapping the words of the other person. In informal communication, people do not like to sit and listen to complete sentences.

Written English, on the other hand, is based on complete sentences set down in orderly fashion with the observance of correct capitalization and punctuation. (Communication on the Internet is totally outside the province of this manual.) Every written sentence is expected to begin with the capitalization of the first word. (We do not begin a sentence with digits or a symbol as in "49 persons were injured in the accident" or "& is the symbol for 'and.'" We would write "Forty-nine persons were injured in the accident." If the number required more than two words, we would arrange it so that the number appeared somewhere else in the sentence, as "The number of persons injured in the accident reached 249." Similarly, the symbol would be placed somewhere else in the sentence, as "The symbol for 'and' is &."

Every written sentence is expected to end with a period if it is a statement, a question mark if it is a question, and an exclamation point if it is an exclamation. Under no circumstances would an adult writer use more than one exclamation point for a sentence.

It is also expected that all words will be spelled correctly, a goal more easily reached nowadays with the Spell Check on computers. Conforming to these basic requirements goes a long way toward creating a good impression even before the reader's eyes have reached the final word.

Confidence in writing good sentences comes from knowing their anatomy. Just as beginning medical students spend time in the dissecting room in order to learn all the parts of human bodies, so a beginning writing student would do well to spend time dissecting sentences in order to learn all their parts. Then he or she would be able to recognize and repair faulty sentences as well as compose new ones that were varied as well as correct. The possibilities for variety and effectiveness are many.

Composing a basic English sentence is a simple matter of arranging a few essentials in any one of seven possible ways. But that is only the beginning. Most sentences, even in everyday writing, need to have details added in one way or another. They also need to be transformed out of their basic flat-footed version in order to serve different purposes. It is what the writer does when handling the additions and variations that matters.

The basic sentence is simple (just one subject and verb), declarative (makes a statement), active (non-passive), and non-negative. Long complicated statements and arguments are transformations of basic sentences. Questions, commands, and exclamations are transformations. Negative or emphatic sentences are transformations. Sentences with their normal word order changed -- the normal subject word either deleted or moved to an inconspicuous position—are transformations. (These sentences are called "passives"—a term to be explained later.) Modern language theory holds that all transformations are derived from basic statements subconsciously in ways that need not concern us at this stage.

Language, like music, has overtones, Some of these can reveal the mood and even the purpose of the writer or speaker. When a sentence is spoken, the voice helps to convey attitude. We might be talking to a disinterested teen-age son or trying to project an in-charge image of ourselves or hoping to appeal to the listener's better nature or giving way to an emotion such as anger. (The range is almost unlimited— formality, hostility, urgency, humor, annoyance, emphasis, pathos, self-pity, authority, etc.) In a written sentence the overtones are more subtle. They can be revealed by word choice, wordiness or concision, presence or absence of detail, and use of rhetorical devices, as well as the actual skeletal structure of the sentence.

The following sentences suggest the wide variety possible when the basic sentence is manipulated. We do not even need to hear the tone of voice or see the facial expression of the speaker--

You walk dog. (basic sentence)

I want you to walk the dog.
I wish you would walk the dog.
Walk the dog (please).
Will you walk the dog?
Would you please walk this dog?
I wish somebody here would walk the dog.
It would be nice if you walked the dog.
Are you going to walk the dog or not?
Is it such a big thing to ask—that you walk the dog?
Why do I always end up walking the dog?
Is anybody going to walk the dog?
I hate being the dog-walker all the time.
It's dog-walk time, Sweetie.
Do me a favor and walk the dog.
That computer game can wait; the dog can't.
I'd be happy to let someone else walk the dog.
If you loved me, you'd walk the dog.
If you loved the dog, you'd walk him once in a while.

The following series is another illustration of what can be done starting with a simple sentence.

Basic sentence—Mr. Brillo dropped the piano. (Brillo dropped piano)

The piano was dropped by Mr. Brillo.

The piano was dropped.
Mr. Brillo did not drop the piano.
Mr. Brillo didn't drop the piano, did he?
Mr. Brillo did so drop the piano.
The piano was not dropped by Mr. Brillo.
The piano was dropped by Mr. Brillo, wasn't it?
The piano was not dropped by Mr. Brillo, was it?
Mr. Brillo dropped the toy piano. (A second sentence—" piano was toy"—was collapsed into one word--"toy"-- to be inserted into the first sentence.)
Mr. Brillo dropped the piano and Rosie screamed. (a second sentence added)
What did Mr. Brillo drop?
Who dropped Mr. Brillo's piano?
Did Mr. Brillo drop the piano?
What was dropped by Mr. Brillo?.

We can also shrink this basic sentence into a smaller unit in order to insert it into a second sentence—
The dropping of the piano (was an accident).
(We were all shocked by) Mr. Brillo's dropping of the piano.
For Mr. Brillo to drop the piano (was inexcusable).
(I hope) Mr. Brillo's piano-dropping (doesn't become a habit).

The starting point on the way to achieving this much control over our sentences is a mastery of the simple basic structure . Think of the basic structure as the bare bones of the sentence. All sorts of extras (such as description) may be added, but with any of the bones missing, the sentence will not be acceptable because it will be defective. In the following pages we will dissect sentences to see what kind of bone structure they have and what kinds of extras have been added.
Even if a sentence contains an error in usage—failure to make the subject and verb agree as to singular or plural, for instance—the sentence communicates its message as long as one of the seven basic patterns has been followed. Incorrect subject-verb agreement would be a mere wrinkle on the surface.

On the other hand, violation of a sentence pattern would result in an unacceptable sentence. Incompleteness of pattern would produce a sentence fragment, and an illegal combination of patterns would produce a run-on sentence. Both are considered serious writing errors because English is a word-order language and tampering with the word order can either confuse the reader or change the meaning of the sentence. ("The dog bit the cat" is very different from "The cat bit the dog").

TABLE OF CONTENTS

CHAPTER 1

VERB POWER
The Seven Sentence Patterns

A. Fish swim--2 elements
B. Heat melts ice--3 elements
C. Mama gave Eddie (a) cookie--4 elements
D. (The) delegates named Wilson chairman--4 elements
   Jane dyed (her) scarf blue--4 elements
E. Australia is (a) continent--3 elements
F. Oceans are salty--3 elements
G. (The) taxi is here--3 elements
   (The) time (to act) is now--3 elements

Each of the sentences A-G represents a different underlying pattern. Each sentence is a simple statement, the rock bottom unit of writing. We can add other words to these basic patterns and we can combine them in many different ways, but we cannot omit any essential element. When sentences like these appear, they are called "simple sentences." They are also known as "independent clauses," meaning that they can stand alone as grammatically correct . (We'll see later on that they are the foundation upon which we build complicated supersentences.)

Notice that not one word in these sentences (except the words in parentheses) can be dropped without leaving the message incomplete. (The words "a, an, the" are little servant words that have no grammatical significance. Other servant words will also be enclosed in parentheses, indicating that they can be dropped without affecting the grammatical requirements of the sentence).
A sentence often contains extra words that disguise the basic pattern by adding descriptive details that are interesting. These will be discussed in future chapters. For now, however, we'll be concentrating on simple sentences. They consist of just one subject -verb combination.

Subject and Verb

Every basic sentence, no matter what pattern it represents, must begin the same way--a noun (or noun substitute)--called the Subject--followed by a verb. It is not until we go past the verb that differences occur. This is due to the nature of verbs. They are the most powerful of all sentence elements. They cooperate with the subject noun (e.g. Does the subject noun want a singular or plural verb?) and then they control what comes next. They may not require anything to follow or they may demand one or even two elements to follow.

The verb standing alone or in combination with modifiers or other elements is called " the predicate." Thus we can say that a simple sentence consists of a subject (noun) and a predicate (verb with or without any following elements).

Sentence A illustrates the minimum, while sentences B-C-D-E-F-G show what can be added. We always have a sequence--Whom or what we are talking about? (the subject) and What happened? (the verb). (In more complicated sentences, the subject and verb do not always come first, but for the present we will be dealing only with simple sentences that begin with subject + verb.)

Nouns

Nouns are the second most important sentence element and the only element that can send a substitute (called a Pronoun) to do its job.

A noun is usually defined as "a person, place, or thing." It is all those and more. It can be the name for a piece of reality (Mr. Jones, gun, Paris, breakfast). This can be called "the reality referent." It can be the name for a state of mind or emotion (anger, confusion). It can be the name for something produced by the mind (goblin, idea, answer). It can be the name of a process (oxidation). A noun answers the question Who? or What ?(For categories and forms of nouns, see Appendix A. The category a noun belongs to --e.g. count or non-count--does not affect its basic function as an element in a sentence pattern.)

Nouns work at the following jobs--
1. Subject of the verb (the doer of the action or the focus of the sentence). In basic sentences this noun precedes the verb.
     Fish swim.
2. Direct Object of the verb (the receiver of the action). In basic sentences this noun follows the verb.
     Heat melts ice.

3. Indirect Object--a noun--(the person or thing that benefits from the verb action.) An indirect object never occurs without a direct object, but a direct object often occurs without an indirect object. In basic sentences the indirect object noun stands between the verb and the direct object.

> Mama gave Eddie (a) cookie.

4. Objective Complement (the re-namer of the direct object). After certain verbs, where there is a direct object, a second noun renaming the object, follows immediately.

> (The) delegates named Wilson chairman.

Nouns do two other jobs when working with linking verbs. These will be discussed further on in this chapter. One more job does not involve verbs and will be discussed in Chapter 3.

Importance of Nouns

It should be remembered that nouns, as well as verbs, are major parts of the sentence and cannot be dropped without damaging the sentence structure. There are two exceptions--

1. a noun working as object of a preposition. Here it is just a part of a modifying, hence droppable, phrase. (See Chapter 3).
2. a noun that has been made into a possessive so that it can modify another noun (Mary--Mary's car). In this case it has been demoted to the status of an adjective and therefore has become a servant word.

Noun Substitutes--Pronouns

Sometimes a noun is replaced by a substitute to avoid repetition.
" Maria sprained Maria's ankle" becomes "Maria sprained her ankle."
" Maria refused to see a doctor" becomes "She refused to see a doctor."
A noun substitute is called a Personal Pronoun. It belongs to a small group of words that exist solely to replace nouns--

> I, my, mine, me, you, yours, he, his, him, she, her, hers, it, its, we, our, ours, us, they, their, theirs, them

The different forms of these busy little words convey information about person (first, second, third), number (singular or plural), case (nominative, possessive, objective), and sometimes gender (masculine, feminine, neuter). (See Appendix A.)
The use of a pronoun in a sentence has no effect on the sentence pattern. Since a noun cannot be dropped without damaging the sentence structure, its substitute--the pronoun--also cannot be dropped.

Pronouns at Work

Needless repetition of nouns --Tom saw Jane that morning, but Tom did not see Jane that afternoon.
Pronoun use--Tom saw Jane that morning but he did not see her that afternoon.
Needless repetition of noun--The mayor misplaced the mayor's car keys.
Pronoun use--The mayor misplaced his car keys.
Needless repetition of noun--Harry bought a new boat. That red boat is Harry's.
Pronoun use--Harry bought a new boat. That red boat is his.

First-Person, Second-Person, and Third-Person Pronouns

Before we think about using the case forms of pronouns correctly when writing, we need to make an overall decision about person--first, second, or third.

Writing in the first person means that the sentences are subjective rather than objective. Over and above the information being conveyed, the sentences focus attention on the speaker --"I believe..." "It seems to me..." Sometimes an emotion such as regret is revealed-- "How can we not mourn for..."
The effect is achieved by the use of certain pronouns--"I,, my, mine, me, we, our, ours, us." The reader feels that the writer is communicating directly with him or her. "I think we can all agree that the tax rate is a problem." This creates a sense of intimacy which can be disliked by a reader who is not a friend or acquaintance.

Using the pronouns "you, your, yours" puts the writing into the second person.
This often makes the writer sound authoritative or superior, a situation that offends the average American, particularly if the word "you" is combined with the word "should." "You should favor a lower tax rate. You should all agree on that."
Writing in the second person is best avoided.

Most writers use the third person by means of the pronouns "he, his, him, she, her, hers, it, its, they, their, theirs, them." This keeps the reader at a comfortable distance and establishes the more formal impersonal tone that is customary in day-to-day dealings with others. "The voters are in disagreement about the tax rate. They are reluctant to discuss their position."

It is important to be consistent in our use of these pronouns. Mixing the levels can destroy the reader's confidence in the writer's ability to think clearly.

Noun Referents of Pronouns

Since a pronoun is not an independent element like a noun, an isolated pronoun raises questions in the reader's mind. To do its job properly, a pronoun must look back to a previously mentioned or clearly understood noun. Traditional grammar calls this "the antecedent." We call it "the noun referent."

> He went home early because he felt ill.

This sentence is not acceptable. It is obvious that the second "he" is referring to the first "he." However, that first "he" must refer to a previously mentioned noun (which can be in a preceding sentence). If there is no preceding sentence, the first "he" must be replaced by a noun so we understand whom the writer means-

> Mr. Smith went home early because he felt ill.

In a sequence of sentences, the referent is often in the preceding sentence.

> The honored guest at the party was Mr. Jack Ellis. He brought his daughter with him.

"He" looks back to "Mr. Jack Ellis," and the other two pronouns ("his, him") look back to "he," which looks back to "Mr. Jack Ellis." No other noun referring to a male person is allowed to come between "he" and its referent "Mr. Jack Ellis.

> The honored guest at the party was Mr. Jack Ellis accompanied by his twin brother Tom. He brought his daughter with him.

According to this sequence, it was Tom's daughter who came. If we want it to be Jack's daughter, we have to move the reference to the twin brother out of the way

> The honored guest at the party was Mr. Jack Ellis. He brought his daughter with him. He was also accompanied by his twin brother Tom.

In the following sentence sequences we have no reference problem because a difference in gender produces different pronouns..

> The host of the party was Mr. Robert Smith, who was accompanied by his wife. He went home early because he felt ill.

"His" looks back without interruption to "Mr. Robert Smith," and "He" obviously refers to the male person.

> The host of the party was Mr. Robert Smith, who was accompanied by his wife. She went home early because she felt ill.

"She" obviously refers to the female person.

The difference in pronoun forms for singular and plural can also eliminate the reference problem.

> The members of the audience enjoyed the leading man's performance. They gave him a standing ovation.

Obviously, "They" does not look back to "leading man." It looks back to "members."

Sometimes a sequence omits the noun referent entirely and becomes an unacceptable sentence---

> Plans for the new bridge caused an uproar in the town. They objected to the high cost.

"They" has no preceding noun referent.

Both the following are acceptable corrections--

> Plans for the new bridge caused an uproar among the townspeople. They objected to the high cost.

"They" now has the preceding noun referent "townspeople."

> Plans for the new bridge caused an uproar in the town. The people objected to the high cost.

The pronoun has been omitted.

Exercise 1

Locate all pronouns and find their noun referents.
1. The Nelsons invited my mother to their party, but she won't go.
2. The beauty queen wore her crown when she went to dinner even though it gave her a headache.
3. The fire had burned its way through the roof before the firefighters could raise their ladders to reach it.
4. The fisherman brought his catch ashore and waited for the spectators to make their purchases.
5. At the theater the ushers did not notice the dog sitting in the back row, although it kept growling at them.

Verb Power

There are two categories of verbs--action verbs and linking verbs. Action verbs produce sentences that are little dramas. Linking verbs produce sentences that resemble equations.

For verb forms--principal parts, tenses, and moods, see Appendix A.

Action Verbs

Without even thinking about it, the native speaker or writer chooses a verb that best conveys his sentence message. Once chosen, the verb's semantic personality controls what sentence elements can come next.

For example, many verbs name an action and then demand mention of the receiver of the action (a following noun).

> (The) hunter shot..
> (The) dog ate..
> Heat melts...

In each of these sequences we expect a third element to complete the message. This is called "the direct object."

> (The) hunter shot (a) rabbit.
> (The) dog ate (my) steak.
> Heat melts ice.

This third element (the direct object) is always a noun or pronoun whose referent (representative in the real world) is different from the noun or pronoun that occupies the subject position. (subjects--"hunter, dog, heat" / direct objects--"rabbit, steak, ice.")

On the other hand, we can have an action verb whose semantic nature does not demand mention of a receiver of the action.

> Fish swim.
> (The) firecracker exploded.
> (The) prisoner escaped.

In the following sentence we have an example of a verb that demands mention of the receiver of the action plus something more--

> Mama gave (a) cookie.

We need to know who or what benefited from the action.

> Mama gave Eddie (a) cookie.

Here we have a direct object --"cookie"--and the beneficiary of the action --"Eddie"-- the indirect object of the verb. Both the direct object and the indirect object will be a noun or pronoun whose real-world referents are different from each other and from the subject.

In these following sentences the verb also demands two following elements--mention of the receiver of the action and mention of something specific about the direct object---

> (The) delegates named ... ...
> (The) delegates named Wilson ...
> (The) delegates named Wilson chairman.

The receiver of the action is the direct object--" Wilson"--and the renaming noun--"chairman"-- is the objective complement because it completes the meaning of the direct object. The direct object and the objective complement will both have the same referent in the real world. "Wilson" and "chairman" name the same person.

 The next sentence is a variation because the objective complement is an adjective rather than a noun. It is telling us something important about the noun.

> Jane dyed (her) scarf...

Jane dyed her scarf blue
The direct object is still a noun--"scarf."

Summary

Unlike linking verbs, which always demand a completer (see following section), an action verb can take a completer or not. When it does take a completer, it is said to be Transitive because it transfers its action to a receiver. This symbolized as "Vtr." When it does not take a completer, it is said to be Intransitive. This is "Vintr."

Transitive--
> The elephant raised his trunk.
> I gave the monkey a banana.
> The guard called me a nuisance.

Intransitive--
> The lion roared.

Very often a sentence with an intransitive verb will end with a descriptive adverb (adverb of manner)--
> The lion roared loudly.

This adverb, of course, is dropped when we reduce the sentence to its basic elements.

Additions to a Sentence Pattern

When a sentence fulfills the requirements of 2, 3, or 4 elements for a particular pattern, then the writer is free to add all sorts of description--
> In all the oceans of the world, fish of many different varieties swim slowly or rapidly in a continual search for food.
> what kind? or which?--of many different varieties
> when?--continual
> where?--in all the oceans of the world
> why?--in a continual search for food
> how?--slowly or rapidly

These details, however, do not affect the grammatical strength of the sentence. That strength lies in the necessary noun and verb combinations that are specified in the seven basic sentence patterns.

Symbols for Noun Positions in Action-Verb Sentences

Symbols enable us to see referential differences and required word order at a glance. English is a word-order language, and a violation of the required word order can change the meaning of the sentence.
In dealing with a basic sentence (all modifying words deleted), we have 4 possible noun positions in an action-verb sentence. Only three of these positions can be filled in any one sentence.

First position = subject. This is symbolized by N-1. It is always filled. All other noun positions (second, third, fourth) follow the verb. Sometimes there are no nouns in any of these post-verb positions, as in "Birds sing." This is symbolized as N-1 + Vintr + ___ + ___ + ___ (The verb action is not transferred.)

Post-Verb Noun Positions

a) two nouns following the verb--

      The guide gave the tourist a map.

 Basic version--

      Guide gave tourist map. N-1 + Vtr + N-2 + N-3 + ___

Not only do these 3 nouns stand in 1-2-3 order, they also have different referents--"guide," "tourist," and "map" are three different pieces of reality.

N-2 is working as the indirect object and N-3 is working as the direct object.

b) two nouns following the verb--

      Tom named his dog Barker.

 Basic version--

      Tom named dog Barker. N-1 + Vtr + ___ + N-3 + Nn-3

In this pattern we do not have an indirect object. We have a final noun with the same referent as the direct object. It is the objective complement. This sentence is dealing with only two pieces of reality-- Tom and his dog. We use Nn-3 to indicate that it is a different word from the N-3 word.

If the N-2 (indirect object) position is filled, the Nn-3 (objective complement) position will be empty and vice versa.

c) one noun following the verb--

      Mrs. Watson drives a big truck.

Basic version--

      Mrs. Watson drives truck N-1 + Vtr + ___ + N-3 + ____

This sentence has just a direct object.

Summary

There are three post-verb positions for nouns, and all can be empty if we have an intransitive verb: N-1 + Vintr + ____ + ____ + ____.

If we have a transitive verb, at least one of the positions will be filled: N-1 + Vtr + ____ + N-3 + _____.

Two of the positions can be filled, but all three cannot be filled.

N-1 + Vtr + N-2 + N-3 + ____

N-1 + Vtr + ___ + N-3 + Nn-3

Exercise 2

Using symbols as above, label all the noun positions in the following sentences. Remember to delete all modifiers first so that we are dealing with the basic sentence patterns.
1. A famous architect designed the new library.
2. Engineers gave the bridge a rigorous inspection.
3. His fame spread little by little.
4. Few city children play traditional sidewalk games.
5. Our mayor handed the new champion a silver trophy.
6. A nightly fireworks show dazzled spectators.
7. The new law made elderly citizens honorary senators.
8. The committee elected Mr. Perkins temporary chairman.
9. Dorothy's father suddenly disappeared.
10. Our cat brought my mother a dead mouse.

Linking Verbs

Some sentences have entirely different patterns because the verb in each case is a different kind of verb. Instead of action that is transferred, we have an equation. The verb--usually "be"--links the noun subject on the left of the verb with a key word on the right side of the verb. There is never any action.

Every sentence with a linking verb has 3 and only 3 positions, all of which must be filled. We symbolize "linking verb" as "Vlink."

N-1	Vlink	Key Word
Australia	is	(a) continent
Australia = continent		
Oceans	are	salty
Oceans = salty		
(The) taxi	is	here
(The) taxi = here		
(The) time	is	now
(The) time = now		

The key word will be any one of three possibilities--
1. Predicate Noun-- noun that renames the subject noun. In the first sentence "continent" renames "Australia." It has the same referent as the subject noun, but is a different word. There is only one piece of reality being mentioned. Therefore the N-1 symbol of the subject is repeated but with a variation to show that it is a different word--Nn-1.

N-1 (subject)	Vlink	Nn-1 (Predicate Noun)
Australia	is	continent

Predicate Pronoun--Once in a while the position of the predicate noun is occupied by a pronoun. It will always be a possessive form ("mine, yours, his, hers, its, ours, theirs") that refers to the subject noun.

        (My bicycle)--That bicycle is mine. (bicycle = mine)
        (Your book)--This book is yours. (book = yours)
        (His shoes)-- Those shoes are his. (shoes = his)
        (Her castle)-- The castle was hers. (castle = hers)
        (Our furniture)--The furniture on the first floor is ours. (furniture =ours)
        (Their chairs)-- The chairs on the second floor are theirs. (chairs =theirs)

Notice the different spelling of some of the pronouns.

2. Predicate Adjective-- adjective that describes the subject noun

N-1	Vlink	Pred Adj
Oceans	are	salty

3. Predicate Adverb/pl,t--an adverb of place or time that describes the subject noun (No other kind of adverb can do this job.)
In the following sentences, "here," an adverb of location, and "now," an adverb of time, act as Predicate Adverbs.

N-1	Vlink	Pred Adv pl/t
taxi	is	here
time	is	now

The verb "be" always acts as a linking verb. Other verbs that sometimes (but not always) act like linking verbs include "appear, become, feel, grow, look, seem, smell, taste, turn" when they are followed by a predicate adjective.

        (The) child appeared happy / child = happy
        (My) friend became angry / friend = angry
        (The) corn grew tall / corn = tall
        (The) referee looked confused / referee = confused
        (The) referee seemed confused / referee = confused
        (The) soup smelled good / soup = good
        (The) cake tasted delicious / cake = delicious
        (The) milk turned sour / milk = sour

Exercise 3

In the following sentences, label each verb "action tr" or "action intr" or "link," enclose unnecessary words in parentheses, and label each sentence element.

Examples--	N-1	action verb Vtr	N-2	N-3
	(My) uncle	gave	(the) house	(a) (fresh) coat (of paint).

N-1	Vlink		Nn-1
(His) grandfather	is	(a) (successful)	lawyer

1. An astronaut walked on the moon.
2. The old violinist played a solo.
3. Our new business was successful.
4. A beautiful voice made the young singer famous.
5. A low-sodium diet is a sensible choice.
6. The children called the new puppy Brownie.
7. A dealer sold my brother a cheap car.
8. Some people walk very slowly.
9. My professor was a certified expert.
10. The bandleader is right here.

Reminder--Words or groups of words that answer any of the following questions are unnecessary and should be enclosed in parentheses-- What kind, size, color...? Which one?, Whose?, When?, Where?, Why?, How? (It can be helpful to think of these words as members of a WH- Club with "How" as the odd member. They all ask unnecessary questions and all can be discarded.)

If a word is acting as a necessary sentence element, it cannot be dropped. For example, an adjective preceding a noun is dropped, but a predicate adjective or an adjective acting as an objective complement (Nn-3) must be kept. Most adverbs are dropped, but a predicate adverb of place or time after a linking verb must also be kept.

No matter how detailed the sentence may be, if one of the necessary elements is missing, it becomes a Sentence Fragment. This is considered a writing error.

Reminder--A noun is the only part of speech that can have a substitute (a pronoun). Verbs, adjectives, and adverbs cannot. A pronoun makes it unnecessary to repeat the noun. A pronoun is identified symbolically as a noun (N-1. etc.). It never has a modifier.
A noun in the possessive form works as an adjective and is dropped when we look for required elements. Similarly, a possessive pronoun acting as an adjective is dropped unless it is working as a predicate adjective after a linking verb.

The mechanic changed Mike's tire. (We drop "Mike's.")

N-1	Vtr	N-3
mechanic	changed	tire

That coat is hers. ("Hers" is working as a predicate adjective and is not dropped.)

N-1	Vlink	Pred. Pronoun
coat	is	hers

Exercise 4

Put the correct symbol above each of the required elements in the following sentences. Put parentheses around words that are not required elements. Do not indicate empty positions. Label as "Fragments" all sentences missing a required element .
Examples--

N-1 .	Vtr		N-3
Maria	sprained	(her)	ankle
N-1	Vtr	N-2	N--3
Joe	gave	me	(a) wink

1. In the trash I found an old photograph album.
2. A long trail through an evergreen forest near the coast of northern Oregon.   .
3. An attendant finally scrubbed the floor clean.
4. My best friend's father was the speaker at our commencement.
5. The music of a brass band always gives the crowd pleasure.
6. The football team played enthusiastically in spite of the rain.
7. The senior class unanimously made Ed their spokesman.
8. Everyone hoping for sunny weather during our vacation trip.
9. Mrs. Smith was unrecognizable in the dim light of the garage.
10. The usual time for our meeting was noon.

Note—Whether a noun is singular or plural, count or non-count, common or proper makes no difference in its sentence job. It will act as a subject, object of the verb, object of a preposition, or predicate noun regardless of its meaning.

14

CHAPTER 2

SERVANT WORDS FOR NOUNS AND VERBS

Nouns and verbs are the queens and kings of sentences and they have many servants. The servant words provide all the details that make sentences interesting, but they must be dropped if we are examining a sentence to see if the underlying pattern is complete.

.

Noun Servants

Some noun servants precede the noun; others follow the noun. All of them have the job of providing our sentences with details to make our message more accurate and more interesting. However, no noun servant words affect the grammatical status of the sentence. When we are examining the basic sentence pattern, we drop all noun servant words so that the sentence is reduced to its bare bones.

Servant Words That Precede the Noun--
Determiners, Adjectives, Noun Adjuncts

1. DETERMINERS
   a) articles--"a, an, the"
   b) demonstratives--"this, that, these, those"
   c) possessives--"my, your, his, her, its, our, their" and nouns ending in apostrophe + "s."
   d) quantifiers--"one, two, three..., many, more, several, both, all, few, some, every"
   e) negator--"no"

Articles

Articles tell whether the noun is indefinite or definite .
("An" is used when the noun begins with the letter "a.")
> A leaky boat can sink.
> An apple makes a good dessert.

definite--the boat, the apple (one particular boat or apple.)
> The leaky boat finally sank.
> This apple is not ripe.

singular or plural--a boat, an apple (These articles mark a noun as singular.)

boats, apples (To mark the noun as plural, we add "-s" to the noun and drop "a" or "an."

My uncle bought a boat.

People sometimes live on boats.

I bought an apple.

The children were all eating apples.

"The" is used with both singular and plural nouns.

I read the book three times.

The books were on sale.

Proper nouns (always spelled with a capital letter) do not generally require the definite article "the."

Uncle Henry visited London.

(no determiner necessary)

I went to a concert of Beethoven's music.

("I" is a pronoun, not a noun, and therefore does not take a determiner. A pronoun always does its job alone. "Concert" is a common noun and requires a determiner.)

Papa saw two cats on Frank's porch.

("Papa" is a proper noun--no determiner necessary. "Cats" is a common noun and requires a determiner. "Porch" is a common noun and requires a determiner.)

Many proper nouns naming geographic locations or famous institutions idiomatically require the article ":the" and some do not. There is no dependable rule.

Article	No article
the White House	Ellis Island
the United States	Canada
the Statue of Liberty	Disneyland
the Mojave Desert	Great Salt Lake
the Mississippi (river)	Mississippi (state)
the Everglades	Niagara Falls
the Chicago Limited	Amtrak
the Bronx	Brooklyn, Queens, Manhattan, Staten Island
the University of Michigan	New York University
the Long Island Expressway	Northern State Parkway
the United States Senate	Congress

So powerful are articles that putting one in front of any kind of word or even a sign or number turns it into a noun for that one time. It can then be used as subject or object in a sentence

> Every "x" in her handwriting looks like a chicken scratch.
> ("x" is N-1.)

(The quotation marks are required by a punctuation rule and have nothing to do with the grammatical situation.)

> In doing addition, I often skip a 9 or an 8.
> ("a 9 or an 8" is a word group acting as the N-3.)

Demonstratives

> "this, that, these, those"

These words are pointers. They tell whether the noun referent is nearby or at a distance. The first two are used for singular nouns; the second two for plural.

> This seat (nearby) is more comfortable than that seat. (at a distance)
> These strawberries (nearby) are riper than those strawberries. (at a distance)

Possessives --three kinds

1. The first kind of possessive consists of a small group of words which are members of the pronoun family.. With slight changes in form, they can appear in two different sentence positions--preceding a noun or alone in the predicate adjective place.

Possessive pronouns preceding the noun--

> "my"--belonging to the single speaker-- "my dog"
> "your"--belonging to the person addressed --"your dog"
> "her" and "his"--belonging to the person spoken about, showing that   person's gender--"her dog," "his dog"
> "its"--belonging to a non-human--" That noisy car lost its muffler."
> "our"--belonging to more than one speaker--"our house"
> "their"--belonging to more than one person spoken about "The hikers lost their map."

(It is important to remember that these words when used as possessives, as in the sentences above, are never spelled with an apostrophe. That is a common misspelling.)

Possessive pronouns standing alone after the linking verb (always the verb "be") in the predicate adjective position--

> This dog is mine.
> That dog is yours.
> The big dog is hers.

The smaller dog is his.
That house is ours.
The map is theirs.
"Its" is not used in this position.

The ownership pronoun which precedes a noun can be dropped without damaging the sentence pattern, but the ownership pronoun which stands alone in the predicate adjective position cannot be dropped.

Brownie is my dog.   Brownie is dog.
Brownie is mine.   Brownie is ---

2. The second kind of possessive is by far the most common. It consists of a noun to which has been added either an apostrophe or an apostrophe + "-s."
 A singular noun takes apostrophe + "-s" even if it already ends in "s."
A plural noun ending in "s" takes just the apostrophe. A plural noun not ending in "s" is treated like a singular noun.
Singular noun--

Susan's keys are missing.
Tom borrowed Mr. Brown's umbrella.
Charles's face is sunburned.
 Mr. Moss's garden is beautiful.

 Plural noun--

I wrote down the policemen's names.
I wrote down the boys' names.

3. The third kind of possessive is the least common. It is called a "genitive" phrase because it is like a translation from the Latin genitive case. The English equivalent is an "of" phrase--"tusks of an elephant" instead of "elephant's tusks." While the genitive phrase with "of" does exist in English, it is used mostly when referring to the attributes of an animal or an inanimate object. However, the apostrophe + "-s" can also be used. Formal writing gives preference to the genitive phrase. Whenever there is a choice, it is well to keep in mind that an "of" phrase adds an extra word to the sentence. This works against the tendency of contemporary English to reduce wordiness in keeping with the modern preference for speed..

Quantifiers

one, two, three..., many, more, several, both, all, few, some, every

two miles, many students, more freedom, several weeks,
both parents, all passengers, few taxpayers, some cats,
every child

Negators

"neither" (referring to two and often used with the pronoun "one") and
"no"

no job no confidence   no waiting   no fresh fish   no
one
Neither criminal would confess.
Neither one of my children likes broccoli.

The use of the noun "nobody" will also make a sentence negative--
Nobody answered the phone.

2. ADJECTIVES

. describers of color, size, value, shape, material, condition, etc.--
red shirt, large box, priceless tapestry, square window,
silk dress, new house

Comparison of Adjectives

Most descriptive adjectives and adverbs have three forms--positive,
comparative, and superlative. The basic or positive form is always
used unless we are comparing two or more items. If we are comparing
two items, we use the comparative, and if we are comparing three or
more items, we use the superlative.

Positive--Tom is a tall man.
Comparative--Tom is taller than his friend William.
Superlative--Artie is the tallest of the three friends.

Notice that we have added "-er" to the basic form for the comparative
and "-est" to the basic form for the superlative.

long, longer, longest
pale, paler, palest

When the basic form is consists of more than two syllables, the
comparative remains the basic form preceded by "more" and the
superlative remains the basic form preceded by "most."

beautiful, more beautiful, most beautiful
expensive, more expensive, most expensive

Two-syllable adjectives can use either "er/est" or "more/most."

happy, happier, happiest / happy, more happy, most
happy

quiet, quieter, quietest/ quiet, more quiet, most quiet

A few adjectives cannot be compared. because they represent an absolute quality. These include "perfect, unique, pregnant, guilty, innocent."

The use of the superlative form when comparing only two items results in a common grammatical error.

> Wrong--Suzy is the tallest of the twins.
> Correct--Suzy is the taller of the twins.
> Correct--Suzy is the tallest of all three Parker children.

Note--When a sentence is stripped of its nonessentials in order to reveal its basic pattern, the noun possessives are treated like adjectives--that is, they are discarded.

> "The cat's tail is black" becomes "tail is black."
> "Mr. Burns has a boat" reduces to "Mr. Burns has boat.
> "Mr. Burns" is still N-1.

However, if we write" Mr. Burns's boat ran aground," we end up with "boat ran aground." Mr. Burns has disappeared.

Word Order

When there is more than one of the six noun servants to be used, the word order is important. The adjective is always the one closest to the noun.

> a house, an old house, my happy childhood

Sometimes a writer uses two adjectives in front of the noun.

> (the) (four) tall angry fishermen

This is overdoing the description. The writer should choose the more important one and drop the other.

> (A) slender stylish woman (with) blonde curly hair (and)
> (a) warm expansive smile (greeted us.)

This sentence is overloaded with adjectives. Not every single noun in a sentence should have one or two adjectives in front of it. One of the earmarks of bad writing is the overuse of adjectives.

Choice of Adjectives

A good writer does not include adjectives that are irrelevant to the sentence message or which can distract the reader

> A beautiful psychologist took the witness stand.

(The appearance of the psychologist is not important in a courtroom.)

> Our exotic mathematics professor entered the room.

("Exotic" raises a question in the mind of the reader, who wonders what there was about the professor to warrant the use of such an adjective.)

The writer is expected to take time to think of the adjective that most accurately describes the noun in the light of what is being said in the sentence message. If the psychologist were taking part in a beauty contest, the adjective "beautiful" would be appropriate. It is difficult to imagine a sentence message that would make the adjective "exotic" appropriate for the description of a mathematics professor.

Exception--A Special Noun Servant
The Predicate Adjective

Sometimes we drop an adjective and sometimes we don't.

There is one outstanding servant that in one special case steps up to importance as a vital sentence element. This is the adjective. It is most commonly found immediately preceding a noun, as in "sunny day," and we drop it like an ordinary servant when we are looking for the sentence pattern. However, when the adjective stands alone after a linking verb, it is no longer a servant. It is a necessary sentence element called the Predicate Adjective, the third element in the last sentence pattern we met in Chapter I-- N1 + Link Verb + Pred. Adj.

> Skyscrapers are tall.   N1 + Link Verb + Pred. Ad j
> Skyscrapers = tall.

We cannot drop the adjective in this position. It is not a servant here. It is an essential part of the basic sentence. Without it, the sentence equation would not be complete. It is needed to complete the equation formed by the link verb

.

3. NOUN ADJUNCTS

Any noun used descriptively in place of an adjective is called a Noun Adjunct. This usage is a growing trend in English in keeping with the preference for speed and economy of form. When we strip a sentence of modifiers to find the basic elements, we drop the noun adjunct just as we drop adjectives.

> adjective use--a sale of woolen coats
> noun adjunct---a sale of wool coats
> full sentence--The department sale featured wool coats.
> basic elements--store featured coats

The trend toward the use of noun adjuncts is a step away from the more traditional use of a prepositional phrase following the noun--

Traditional--   The door of-the-garage had been left unlocked.
New--   The garage door had been left unlocked.
Traditional--   Our bill for-repairs seemed unreasonable.
New--   Our repair bill seemed unreasonable

Another source of noun adjuncts is an adjective with its characteristic "ed," "en," "al," or apostrophe "s" ending removed.

> orphaned kitten/orphan kitten--The orphan kitten was finally adopted.
> woolen/wool--I bought a red wool coat.
> governmental/ government--Read about the new government regulations.
> doll's/ doll--Jim built his daughter a doll house.

The Pre-Noun Positions

When we wish to use more than one pre-noun servant, we need to pay attention to the order in which we place them. Since English is a word order language, a random placement can produce an unusable sentence. There are six possible positions.

1. negator
>   2. article or demonstrative
>   3. possessive pronoun or noun in possessive form
>   4. quantifier
>   5. adjective (can be more than one)
>   6. noun adjunct

1. not	2. the	3.---	4. two	5. little	6. orphan	kittens
1. not	2. those	3.---	4. two	5. little	6. orphan	kittens
1. not	2. a	3.---	4. ---	5. little	6. orphan	kitten
1. not	2.---	3. my	4. two	5. little	6. orphan	kittens
1. not	2.---	3.---	4. two	5. little	6 orphan	kittens
1. not	2.---	3.Mary's	4. two	5.little gray	6. orphan	kittens

Notice that not all the positions can be filled at any one time.

Post-Noun Modifiers

A good writer is careful not to bury the noun in modifiers. This is particularly true for post-noun modifiers, which always consist of several words packaged as a phrase or dependent clause.

> I saw Mary's two little gray kittens (in-a-yellow-basket) (which someone-had-left- on-her- front-porch).

This is an overloaded sentence.

Sometimes a multi-word modifier can be compressed into a shorter form that allows it to precede the noun--

> Aunt Jane's will mentioned a diamond bracelet (of-her mother's)(that-had -lost-for-many-years).
> Aunt Jane's will mentioned her mother's long-lost diamond bracelet.

Turning the prepositional phrase into a possessive noun makes it an adjective that can precede the noun. The hyphen makes "long" and "lost" into a single word. This sort of compression tightens the sentence, making it much more effective.

Exercise 5

Locate all the pre-noun servants and identify as article, quantifier, negator, demonstrative, adjective, possessive noun, possessive pronoun, noun adjunct, genitive possessive ("of" phrase). Where there is more than one pre-noun modifier, notice the order in which they appear. The one closest to the noun is the most important in terms of the sentence message.

1. A large tree fell on our roof during the violent storm.
2. The storm damage was extensive.
3. Tom borrowed my umbrella and did not return it.
4. No volunteers signed up to put out the sudden fire.
5. We waited for Dorothy's answer to our simple question.
6. The band leader wore a stylish red jacket.
7. Someone stole the new tires off our old car.
8. That muddy dog needs a good bath.
9. Our children never asked the reason for the cancellation of their party.
10. Many spectators carried little flags to wave at their favorite athletes.

Verb Servants

Verb servants are of two kinds--auxiliaries and modals. They always precede the main verb.

1. AUXILIARIES

The verbs "be, have, do" in all their forms can act as main verbs in a sentence or they may act as servants working for another verb. When they serve another verb, they are called auxiliaries.

> The party is a success. "is"--main verb
> The party was canceled. "was"--auxiliary to main verb "canceled"
> Sue danced with her friends. "danced"--main verb
> Sue was dancing with-her-friends. "was"--auxiliary to main verb "dancing"
> Some universities have thousands of-students--"have"--main verb
> Some universities have expanded in-recent-years. "have"-- auxiliary to main verb "expanded"
> My university offered more scholarships.--"offered"--main verb

My university has offered more scholarships. "has"--
auxiliary to main verb "offered"
Tom did his chores every morning--"did"--main verb
Tom does do his chores every morning--"does"-- auxiliary
to main verb "do."

"Be" as an Auxiliary

The verb "be" is used as an auxiliary to a main verb for two different
reasons.
a) It helps the main verb show continued action (and the main verb
must add "ing")

Mother is trying a new recipe. "is" --auxiliary to the main
verb "try." "Ing" is added to the main verb.
Taxes are rising every year. "are"--auxiliary to the main
verb "rise". Main verb is "rise" with added "ing."

b) It is needed to turn the sentence from active to passive. A passive
sentence is a sentence in reverse--the subject is put at the end and the
direct object is put in the subject position. Sometimes the subject is
deleted. In general it is not advisable to write sentences in the passive.

Active (normal) sentence--A stranger witnessed the
crime.
Passive (reversed) sentence--The crime was witnessed
by a stranger.
Passive (reversed) sentence with deleted subject--The
crime was witnessed.

"Have" as an Auxiliary

The verb "have" is used as an auxiliary to a main verb in order to form
two different tenses (See Verbs--Appendix A) and also in order to
make a sentence negative.
Present tense--

My brother takes violin lessons. "takes"--main verb
There is no auxiliary here. The action is simply in the present.
Present perfect tense-- (This really should be called the "present-past"
tense. The word "perfect" means "past." It has nothing to do with
perfection.)

Both my brothers have taken violin lessons for years.
My sister has taken violin lessons for six months.
The auxiliary "have" tells us that the action started in the past and is
continuing in the present. Its singular form is "has."
(The main verb "take" is in its past participle form, which is its
combining form.)
Past perfect tense-- (This really should be called the "past-past"
tense.)

My cousin had taken violin lessons before she started piano.

Here we have two past actions, with one further back in the past than the other.

"Have" with "not" or "never"—

My brother has never taken violin lessons.
My sister has not taken violin lessons.
My cousin had not taken violin lessons before she studied piano.

"Do" as an Auxiliary

When "do" is used as an auxiliary to a main verb, it is because a) we wish to be emphatic or b) we wish to ask a direct question or c) we wish to make the sentence negative.

a) for emphasis (often in reply to a question or a denial)—

Tom did finish his chores. "did" auxiliary to main verb "finish"
Tom did so finish his chores. "did"-- auxiliary to main verb "finish" with "so" added for stronger emphasis. It is only used in spoken arguments.

b) to turn a statement into a direct question—

Tom finished his chores.--Did Tom finish his chores?
Tom dislikes chores--Does Tom dislike chores?

Notice first of all that the added "do" takes on the job of indicating the tense, leaving the main verb in its original infinitive form. Second, the "do" and the subject noun are in reversed order. This is what makes a statement into a question.

In Shakespeare's time, asking a question was easier. The subject word and the verb were simply reversed--"Finished Tom his chores?"

Modern English does not permit this. A form of "do" must be added to the main verb before a reversal can take place.

"Be" is the single exception to this rule. When "be" is the main verb without auxiliary or modal (see Modals below), we can simply reverse subject and verb.

The tiger is a fierce animal.--Is the tiger a fierce animal?
The exams were unusually difficult.--Were the exams unusually difficult?

If any verb already has an auxiliary or a modal, that will permit a reversal without further addition.

The players have gone home.--Have the players gone home?
They were practicing all afternoon.--Were they practicing all afternoon?
We can win this election.--Can we win this election?

c) to make a sentence negative--

Tom finished his chores. Tom did not finish his chores.

Using "do" as an auxiliary to the main verb is necessary in most cases when we wish to add "not."

Exceptions--When "be" is the main verb, "not" can be added without "do."

Tom is a good worker. Tom is not a good worker.

When "have" is the auxiliary of a different main verb, "not" can be used without "do."

Your subscription has expired.--Your subscription has not expired.

("Not" is often contracted to "n't" in informal writing and speaking.)

Tom isn't a good worker.

Your subscription hasn't expired.

More About Auxiliaries

A main verb can have one or two verb auxiliaries.

One auxiliary--

The children have gone indoors.--"have" is auxiliary,
"gone" is main verb.

Two auxiliaries--

The children had been playing soccer--"had" and "been"
are auxiliaries and "play" is main verb.

Auxiliary with Its twin--

When "be", "have" and "do" are acting as main verbs, they can use a twin as their auxiliary.--

My dog is playful. (no auxiliary)

My dog is being playful.

"Is" acts as auxiliary, "being" is main verb ("is" and "being" are forms of the verb "be.")

The town has traffic problems. (no auxiliary)

The town has had traffic problems for-a-long-time.

"Has" is the auxiliary, "had" is the main verb. ("has" and "had" are forms of the verb "have.")

My dog does tricks. (no auxiliary)

My dog does not do tricks.

"Does" is the auxiliary, "do" is the main verb.

("does" and "do" are forms of the verb "do.")

2. MODALS

A group of other verb servants known as Modals in the present and past tense indicate shades of meaning for the main verb. Unlike the three verb/auxiliaries "be, have, do," modals can never act alone. They must always be followed by a main verb. In casual conversation the main verb can be omitted if it is understood, but this is not the case in written English.

Modals--can/could, may/might, must/had to, ought to, 'll/should, will/would.

Because of language unpredictability, there is much irregularity in their use.

"can/could" express possibility or ability.

> Most musicians can read music.

Present tense of "can" is the modal; main verb is "read"

> My cousin could play the piano at six.

Past tense of "can"; main verb is "play."

Some modals show tense (present and past) as with this one. Some modals do not indicate present tense or past tense at all, as evidenced by "may/might" below.

"may/might" express probability or potential. Formerly "may" also expressed permission, but now that American life has become more casual, this use has disappeared.

> Old-fashioned version--You may borrow my tennis racket.

 Present tense of "may." Main verb is "borrow."

> Modern version--You can borrow my tennis racket.

Present tense of "can." Main verb is "borrow."

> I may go to Europe this summer.

Present tense form of "may." Main verb is "go."

> I might go to Europe this summer.

Past tense form of "may," but obviously it has no connection with real time. There is no logical explanation for this. Main verb is "go."

"must/had to " express necessity or obligation

> The postman must deliver the mail.

Present tense of "must." Main verb is "deliver."

> Last week he had to send a substitute.

Past tense equivalent of "must." There is no explanation for this. Main verb is "send."

"ought to"--obligation.   no past tense form

> The mayor ought to appoint a new police chief.

 Present tense form of "ought to." Main verb is "appoint."

"should" indicates obligation.

Although it was the past tense form of "shall"--which was once a modal but now is obsolete--"should" no longer refers to past time. In fact, it operates in the present, as evidenced by the sentence below.

> I should visit my grandmother.

Main verb is "visit."

"will" or its contraction ('ll) helps the main verb form the future tense. Old-fashioned rules once required the use of "shall" for certain fine points of the future tense. That is no longer the case. "Shall" has disappeared.

> Old-fashioned version--I shall see you next week.

Present tense form of "will." Main verb is "see."

> Modern version--I will see you next week.

Present tense form of "will." Main verb is "see."

> I'll see you next week.

Contracted present tense form of "will." Main verb is "see."

"will" also can show determination or promise

> Determination--I will (so) go to the party.

Present tense form of "will." Main verb is "go." The contraction is never used for this meaning.

> Promise--I will help you pack the trunk.

Present tense form of "will." Main verb is "pack."

> Promise--I'll help you pack the trunk.

Contracted present tense form of "will." Main verb is "pack."

"would" is the past tense form of "will," but does not always refer to real time.

> I would drive carefully if I were you.

"Would" looks like a past tense form, but obviously is a reference to the future. It is working in a subtle way to support the subjunctive "were." (English uses the subjunctive only for a few constructions indicating a wish or a condition contrary to fact. See Appendix A.)

> Every morning last summer we would eat breakfast outdoors.

Past tense form of "will" to show habitual action in the past. Main verb is "eat."

> We would have eaten dinner there too if mother had agreed.

Past tense form of "will" + auxiliary "have" + past participle of main verb "eat."

Negatives--Summary

Although we have seen that a sentence can be made negative in the noun area by using a negative noun or noun modifier, the most common way is to add "not" ("n't") or "never" in the verb area. Auxiliaries and modals play a large part in this process. Sometimes we simply add "not" ("n't") or "never," but sometimes we have to add a form of "do," "have" or one of the modals.

Note--"Not" and "never" are actually adverbs-- verb servants like other adverbs, but their placement in regard to the verb is complicated enough to justify separate treatment.

1. Noun area--
  a) negative noun—
        Nobody swims in this pool.
  b) negative modifier—
        No swimmer uses this pool.

2. Verb area--
  a) nothing added except "not, n't, or "never" when "be" is the main verb—
        I am hungry/ I am not hungry.
  b) addition of auxiliary or modal—
        My aunt drives an expensive car/ My aunt has never driven a car.
        The coach blew his whistle/ The coach did not blow his whistle.
        The new tenant paid his rent/ The new tenant could not pay his rent.
        It might rain tomorrow/ It might not rain tomorrow.
        Drivers must use the new bridge/ Drivers must not use the new bridge.
        We ought to pay higher taxes/ We ought not to pay higher taxes.
        You should read more books/ You should not read more books.
        This fabric will fade in the sun/ This fabric will not fade in the sun.

When the main verb is preceded by a modal, the negative word comes between them.
        My brother cannot play the guitar.
        Henry might not buy a car..
        A traveler should not lose his passport.
        I will not go on a diet.

When there are two or three servant words (modal and auxiliaries) preceding the main verb, the negative word is placed after the first servant word—
        auxiliary + not + auxiliary + main verb—
        The children had not been playing soccer.
        The children hadn't been playing soccer.
        modal + auxiliary + auxiliary + main verb—
        The missing book might not have been stolen.
        The missing book mightn't have been stolen.

Exercise 6

Locate and label all auxiliaries and modals.
1. Our tax rate has increased alarmingly this year.
2. Many of us do not learn a new language easily.
3. A cook should sharpen his knives frequently.
4. That icy sidewalk could have caused an accident.
5. The train will have gone by the time I arrive at the station.
6. The boys may have been secretly rehearsing a new stunt.
7. The management is doing a good job this season.
8. Someone ought to help those stranded passengers.
9. We don't know who might have deliberately caused the damage.
10. Large crowds often collected to see the fireworks.

Verb Particles

Often the verb in a sentence is followed by a small word that has no grammatical significance. It is not any kind of object and yet it is not any kind of servant such as an auxiliary or modal. Although it is written as a separate word, it is part of the verb and is pronounced in the same breath as the verb. It can affect verb meaning and cannot be dropped. It is called a Verb Particle. Connecting the verb and its particle with a hyphen would be helpful, but unfortunately that is not done. Any verb + particle combination can be replaced by a one-word verb synonym.

> The investor looked into the financial scheme.
> The investor investigated the financial scheme.
> looked into = investigated
> The detective looked over the crime scene.
> The detective inspected the crime scene.
> looked over = inspected

There are two kinds of verb particles--
a) intensifier
b) meaning changer

a) Intensifier--The word "up" is frequently added to a verb to intensify meaning. This is particularly true in spoken English. The word "up" in these cases is completely meaningless.

> Eat your carrots. / Eat up your carrots.
> A bully beat the new boy. / A bully beat up the new boy.
> Hurry downstairs. / Hurry up and come downstairs.
> I had to add the numbers twice. / I had to add up the numbers twice.

b) Meaning changer-- Many words which normally act as prepositions or adverbs become particles when they are placed immediately after a verb.

> Fred turned down a generous offer for his house ("down" =particle).
> (Fred rejected a generous offer for his house.)
> Santa came down-the-chimney. ("down" is a preposition forming a unit with the words "the chimney." There is no particle here.)
> I put my pencil down. (no particle--"down" is an adverb telling Where)

Exercise 7

Locate all verb particles and write in a one-word substitute for the verb + particle combination.
1. A fire burned up the evidence.
2. A fire burned down the barn.
3. The parade disappeared down the road.
4. My dog chased my cat up a tree.
5. Mary's mother threw out her daughter's old shoes.
6. The little boy wanted to stay outside, but his mother wanted him to come inside.
7. In single file we walked through the tunnel.
8. The play's director ran through the script with the cast.
9. The teacher decided to look over my homework.
10. My neighbors planned to look up some old friends.

Less Important Verb Servants--Adverbs

The large group of words known as adverbs is a collection of servant words that do a variety of jobs. Some of them serve adjectives, some of them serve other adverbs, some of them serve the complete sentence, and some of them serve the individual verb. It is those that serve the verb that concern us here.

Description and other details about verbs are provided by adverbs. These can be individual words or they can be word groups. All answer the questions When? Where? Why? How? How long? How often? To what extent?

Adverbs play no part in the sentence pattern and therefore are droppable when we strip a sentence down to its basic elements. The one exception is the adverb of time or place that follows a linking verb. Again, as with adjectives, when we drop adverbs, we often drop the most interesting part of the sentence. This has to do with meaning. However, we are not concerned with meaning; we are concerned with underlying structure.

Adverbs come in eight varieties—
> 1. Frequency-- My father often walks to work.
> 2. Manner--The dancers moved gracefully across the floor.
> 3.Time--I'll have a talk with you later.
> 4. Degree--The teacher spoke rapidly.
> 5. Place--Because of the rain, the children played inside.
> 6. Negation--Those peaches are not ripe.

"Never"--a frequency adverb--can also make the sentence negative.
> The postman never delivers mail on Sundays.
> 7. Editorial comment--Surprisingly, no winners were announced.

(This kind of adverb tells the reader or listener how the author of the sentence feels about the event described in the sentence. Adverbs like this play no role in the grammatical structure.)
> 8. Transitional--However, the chairman refused to talk to the press.

(This kind of adverb is used only in a sequence of sentences to guide the reader through various steps of an argument or explanation. It plays no role in the grammatical structure.)

Placement of Adverbs
With One-Word Verbs

Unlike adjectives that must always stand in front of the noun they describe, certain types of adverbs are movable. Generally--not always--there are two or three places in the sentence where the writer can choose to put the adverb. While adverbs are generally placed immediately before or after the main verb, they often can also stand at the beginning or end of the entire sentence. The choice of position depends upon the writer's preference. (See Chapter 8.)

The following sentences illustrate some alternate positions.
Frequency—
> Often my father walks to work.
> My father walks to work often.
> My father often walks to work.
> (My father walks often to work--not acceptable)

Manner--
> Gracefully the dancers moved across the floor.
> The dancers gracefully moved across the floor.
> The dancers moved across the floor gracefully.

Time--
>   Later I'll have a talk with you.
>   I'll have a talk with you later.

Degree--
>   The teacher spoke quite rapidly.
>   The teacher spoke too rapidly.
>   The teacher spoke very rapidly.
>   (Adverbs of degree, such as "quite, too, very" always
>   precede the adverb of manner. They cannot be moved.)

Place—
This kind of adverb must follow the main verb or verb-object combination.
>   Sit here. Put the table there. I left my car key inside.
(No alternate positions.)

Editorial comment—
Only in rare instances would this kind of adverb be moved away from the start of the sentence.
>   Fortunately we did not exceed our budget limitation.

Transitional—
This kind of adverb generally begins the sentence, although in some cases it can follow the subject noun.
>   However, the chairman refused to talk to the press.
>   The chairman, however, refused to talk to the press.

Placement of Adverbs with Verb Phrase

Normal position with a verb phrase—
>   The train must have stopped suddenly. (modal + auxiliary
>   + main verb + adverb)

Putting the adverb after the modal can produce an awkward sentence
>   The train must suddenly have stopped.

Putting it after the auxiliary and before the main verb is almost as awkward.—
>   The train must have suddenly stopped.

The best place for the adverb is after the verb.

Placing of the adverb is important when the verb is followed by one or more essential elements such as—
>   direct object (N-3)
>   indirect object+ direct object (N-2 + N-3)
>   direct object + objective complement (N-3 + Nn-3)
>   predicate noun (Nn—1)
>   predicate adjective

verb + direct object + adverb (Vtr + N-3 + adv)
> The decorator measured the window carefully.

adverb + verb + direct object (adv + Vtr + N-3)
> The decorator carefully measured the window.

(We never separate the main verb from its object.)

auxiliary + adverb + main verb + direct object (aux +adv + Vtr + N-3)
> The decorator had carefully measured the window.

auxiliary + main verb + direct object + adverb (aux + vtr + N-3 + adv)
> The decorator had measured the window carefully.

adverb + main verb + indirect object + direct object (adv + Vtr + N-2 + N-3)
> Aunt Emma cheerfully gave Tommy a cookie.

main verb + indirect object + direct object + adverb (Vtr + N-2 + N-3 + adv)
> Aunt Emma gave Tommy a cookie cheerfully.

(We never separate the indirect object from the direct object.)

verb + direct object + objective complement + adv (Vtr + N-3 + Nn-3 + adv)
> The teacher named Rose the winner immediately.

adv + verb + direct object + objective complement (adv+ Vtr + N-3 + Nn-3)
> The teacher immediately named Rose the winner.

(We never separate the direct object from the objective complement.)

Word-Groups Doing Adverb Jobs

> Mr. Hopkins raises mink (for-profit). "For-profit" tells Why.
> Mr. Hopkins raises mink (because-they-are-profitable).
> Why

These adverb word groups are dropped when the sentence is reduced to its basics--

> Mr. Hopkins raises mink. (N-1 + Vtr + N-3)

Note--Occasionally there will be an adverb of time or place standing alone after a linking verb (just as a predicate adjective does). In this case, it cannot be dropped; it is a basic element. (Remember that a linking verb creates an equation, which must have three items.)

> The best time to study is now. "Now" tells When.
> time is now (N-1 + Vlink + adv/t) (adverb of time)
> The best place to study is here. "Here" tells Where.
> place is here (N-1 + Vlink + adv/pl) (adverb of place)

This adverbial use does not occur very often. When it does, the post-verb adverb can be the word package known as a prepositional phrase. (See Chapter 3.)

His summer cabin is in-the-woods.
Word group tells Where.

cabin is in-the-woods (N-1 + Vlink + adv/pl)

Exercise 8

Locate all adverbs and label them according to the eight classifications. Some necessary punctuation has been omitted.

1. The sales clerk often appeared rather sleepy as he carefully wrapped our purchases.
2. The site of a famous battle is here where young men play soccer continually.
3. City authorities however are totally ignorant of the misuse of the carefully tended lawn.
4. Unfortunately my bus did not arrive before the rain had thoroughly soaked my overcoat.
5. The customer who had been waiting nearly an hour for service indignantly announced he was leaving immediately.

.

CHAPTER 3

WORD PACKAGES AS SERVANTS
Minor League---Phrase, Pair/Series, Cluster

We have been dealing with basic sentences. Now it is time to examine sentences that give us more information than just bare facts. English has many ways in which we can include details. We need to see how this is done.

Many details are simply one-word adjectives or adverbs—
> The angry bear growled menacingly.
> basic sentence--bear growled

"Angry" is an adjective (tells which bear) and "menacingly" is an adverb (tells how he growled). However, a detail can consist of several words acting as a unit, which we will call a word package.
> The bear with-the-scarred-face growled at-his-keeper.
> basic sentence--bear growled

In this sentence we have an adjective package describing the bear (with-the-scarred-face) and an adverb package describing his growl (at-his-keeper).

Though we may read a sentence one word at a time occasionally, we are more often apt to be scanning a collection of word packages. Some of the word packages are small and some are large; some are simple and some are complicated. Many of the larger packages contain smaller packages so that we have a Russian-doll effect—one inside the other. The reverse is also true. A small package—in terms of its grammatical importance—can contain a large –more important— package, as we'll see further on.

Each package, big and small, acts like a single word—as if it were a simple noun, adjective, verb, or adverb. Most packages are recognizable by their first word.

Major League and Minor League

Packages can be major league or minor league. Major League packages are those with greater grammatical importance. This means that they contain a subject-verb construction. They are dependent clauses—sentence patterns which have been weakened so that they cannot stand alone. This group includes subordinate clauses, relative clauses, and indirect (buried) questions. (See Chapter 4.)

Minor league packages are of several varieties--phrases, pair/series, and clusters.

First Word Package--Phrases

A phrase is a group of words acting as a minor grammatical unit. It can act as a noun, adjective, or adverb, but it cannot stand alone. It must be part of a sentence pattern.

The "angry bear" sentence above with or without its modifiers can stand alone ("bear growled") because it is a sentence pattern. The following word groups—which we are calling packages because they act as single units-- cannot stand alone. (They would be called Sentence Fragments.)

> with-the-menacing-growl
> showing-its-teeth
> to-feed-the-bear
> teasing-the-bear

Each of these expressions is a type of phrase that must be contained within some kind of sentence pattern.

> I saw the bear with-the-menacing-growl.
> adjective package describing the noun "bear
> I saw the bear showing-its-teeth
> adjective package describing the noun "bear"
> You should not try to-feed-the-bear.
> noun package acting as the direct object of the verb
> Teasing-the-bear is a dangerous activity
> noun package acting as subject of the sentence.

Two Kinds of Phrases

There are two kinds of phrases--those that do not contain a verb (Prepositional Phrases) and those that do contain a verb (Verbal Phrases).

Prepositional Phrases

A prepositional phrase is the simplest and most common. It can be found everywhere in sentences, acting either as an adjective or an adverb. It is always discarded when we strip the sentence down to basics.

Structure

If we take a preposition and put a noun or pronoun after it, we have created a prepositional phrase. The noun or pronoun is called the Object of the Preposition. If we slip any kind of modifier between the preposition and its noun, we have not changed the basic nature of the phrase. We have simply expanded it as though we were stretching a rubber band.

> in school (preposition + noun object)
> in elementary school (preposition + noun modifier + noun object)
> in the new elementary school (preposition + 3 noun modifiers + noun object)
> to me (preposition + pronoun object)
> for them (preposition + pronoun object)

Unlike nouns, pronouns do not have modifiers. Therefore there will never be a, article, quantifier, or adjective between the preposition and its object pronoun.

However, pronouns raise a problem which we do not meet when using nouns.

Pronouns have more than one form depending upon the job they are doing. When they act as subjects or predicate pronouns, they are in the nominative case, and when they act as any kind of object, they are in the objective case.

The objective case forms after a preposition are "me, you, him, her, it, us, them."

(See Appendix A.)

Prepositions

Prepositions are special words that never change appearance and never change their job. Their job is to stand in front of a noun or pronoun and thus form a phrase (which we are calling a package). If a word resembling a preposition is alone in a sentence (not in a package with a noun or pronoun), it is not a preposition; it is a twin word working as an adverb.

> The clock in-the-hall struck eleven.

"In" is a preposition with the noun object "hall" forming the prepositional phrase package that is acting like a single adjective to modify "clock."

> The children came in.

Since the word "in" is not followed by a noun or pronoun object, it is not a preposition. It is an adverb modifying the verb "came."

English has a limited number of prepositions. Although our language keeps adding new nouns, verbs, adjectives, and adverbs, it never adds

any new hard-working words like prepositions, conjunctions, modals,
or auxiliaries.
Prepositions--along with their noun or pronoun objects-- tell
connection, direction, location, or time.

Connection—except, for, like, of, with, without

> except my brother
> for a fee
> like elephants
> of the broom
> with him
> without shoes

Direction—around, down, from, into, over, through, toward, up

> around the castle
> down the stairs
> from Alaska
> into the woods
> over the mountain
> through a tunnel
> toward me
> up the ladder

Location--above, across, against, along, among, at, behind, below,
beneath, beside, between, beyond, by, in, inside, near, off, on, outside,
over, past, under, upon

> above my desk
> across the border
> against the wall
> along a rough road
> among strangers
> at home
> behind us
> below decks
> beneath a blanket
> beside the wounded dog
> between meetings
> beyond the mountains
> by the old mill
> in the pond
> inside the house
> near them
> off the trail

on his head
outside the theater
over the window
past the mall
under the floor
upon a bench

Time—about, after, at, before, during, past, since, till, until

about midnight
after lunch
at noon
before breakfast
during the concert
past two o'clock
since dawn
till evening
until our arrival

A few prepositions come in two or three pieces--along with, by way of, in back of, in front of, in regard to, in spite of, instead of, out of, with respect to

along-with a raincoat
by-way-of the new subway
in-back-of the sofa
in-front-of the car
in-regard-to their jobs
in-spite-of her
instead-of a train
out-of sympathy
with-respect-to the money

Embedding

One prepositional phrase can be part of a larger prepositional phrase. This is called embedding.

at the top of the stairs = 1 large prepositional phrase
"At" is the preposition controlling the entire phrase
"The top of the stairs" is the object of "at." It is a noun unit consisting of article + noun + post-noun modifier (adjectival).This post-noun modifier is a smaller prepositional phrase. (Anything, large or small, that modifies a noun is considered an adjective. Any noun modifier consisting of more than one word generally follows the noun instead of preceding it.)

"of the stairs" is a smaller prepositional phrase

"Of" is the preposition
>"The stairs" is the object of this preposition

The phrase is acting as a unit to modify the noun "top."
>at the top
>of the stairs

Prepositional Phrases as adjectives describing nouns—
>The clock (in-the-hall) struck twelve.
>An employee (with-a-broom) entered the room.
>A house (near-the-river) caught my eye.

They tell Which one, What kind, How many, What color, What shape, etc.

Prepositional phrases as adverbs describing verbs, adjectives, or other adverbs.
>The boy threw the ball (over-the-fence).
>An alarm was sounded (during-the-president's-speech).
>He accepted the award (with-gratitude).

They tell When. Where, Why, How, How often, How long, To what extent.

Single-word adverbs are often movable (adjectives are never movable). Prepositional phrases acting as an adverb package are often movable. While movability is not always 100% successful in terms of ease or awkwardness because of semantic quirks, generally the adverb or adverb package will fit at the beginning of the sentence or at the end—

>The boy threw the ball over-the-fence.-- normal order
>Over-the-fence the boy threw the ball.) unacceptable—creates confusion as to the location of the boy.
>The alarm was sounded during-the-president's-speech.--- normal order
>During-the-president's-speech, an alarm was sounded.— acceptable
>He accepted the award with-gratitude.—normal
>With-gratitude he accepted the award.-- acceptable

Exercise 9

Mark off all prepositional phrases in the following sentences. Be sure to note if a prepositional phrase is embedded in another one. Then label each phrase as adjectival (modifying the noun preceding it) or adverbial (can be located anywhere in the sentence).

1. The watchers at the palace were warned of the spy's approach by a messenger from the sentries outside the city wall.

2. In the living room, Mrs. Field read aloud from the works of Shakespeare while in the kitchen her husband dozed peacefully with a cup of tea on the table in front of him.
3. New arrivals without tickets waited on a long line beside the curb until the people with tickets had been admitted to the inner lobby of the theater.
4. Before her vacation trip, Joan had been anxious about its cost, but during her travels she put all such thoughts out of her mind.
5. Between the two houses strolled a solitary cat with a bandage on its left paw.

Second Word Package--Verbal Phrases
Verbal Noun Phrase, Verbal Adjective Phrase, Infinitive Phrase

Another kind of word package is a verbal phrase whose major ingredient is a verb form. This kind of package comes in three varieties--

1.Verbal Noun Phrase—

jogging-every-day (called a "gerund phrase" in traditional grammar).

This verb form always ends in "-ing." We can take any verb ending in "-ing" and use it as a noun. Traditional grammar then calls it "a gerund." We call it "a verbal noun." It can take adverb modifiers and/or an object or predicate noun complement to form a verbal noun phrase (called traditionally "a gerund phrase").

2. Verbal Adjective Phrase—

recently-polished (called a "participial phrase" in traditional grammar)

This verb form ends in "-ing," "-en," or "-ed." It can be used as an adjective, known in traditional grammar as "a participle." We call it "a verbal adjective." It can take adverb modifiers and/or an object or predicate noun complement. It is then called "a verbal adjective phrase."

3. Infinitive Phrase—

to-buy-a-house (It is almost always introduced by "to.")

The verb in an infinitive phrase is entirely different from the main verb in a sentence. It occurs in a package which can act as a noun or an adjective or an adverb in a sentence. Any basic verb can be turned into an infinitive by preceding it with "to." The infinitive can act as a noun, adjective, or adverb, and it can take adverbial modifiers and/or an object or predicate noun complement.

Verbal Noun Phrases

A Verbal Noun Phrase is a package of words acting as a unit. That unit will be doing any one of the standard jobs of a regular noun--
1. the subject of a verb
2. the object of an action verb
3. the predicate noun after a linking verb
4. the object of a preposition.

1. subject of a verb
> Jogging-every-day is good exercise.
> (Something) is good exercise.

The whole package is the "something"--the subject of the sentence verb.
The verb = "is"
2. object of an action verb
> Susan hated practicing-the-piano.
> Susan hated (something).

The whole package is the "something"--the direct object of the main verb "hated."
3. predicate noun
> Our favorite tradition is decorating-the-Christmas-tree
> Our favorite tradition is (something).

The whole package is the "something"--the predicate noun after the linking verb "is."
4. object of a preposition
> The little boy had a habit of playing-with-matches.
> The little boy had a habit of (something).

The whole package is the "something." It is acting as the object of the preposition "of." The main verb is "had."
 A lone verbal noun can do the same noun job, but of course it is not considered a phrase.
> Jogging is good exercise.
> Susan hated practicing

Internal Structure of Verbal Noun Phrases

Since verbal nouns have the DNA of verbs, they have some of the privileges of verbs even while they are doing a noun job. We refer to them as "verbals" to avoid confusion with the main verb in the sentence.

1. A verbal noun can be modified by adverbs--
> Asking-politely can bring results.

While the whole package (asking-politely) is the subject of the sentence, its internal structure consists of the verbal itself (asking) and its modifying adverb (politely).

2. A verbal noun can take direct objects--

Asking-questions can produce answers.

This package (asking-questions) is the subject of the sentence, but its internal structure consists of the verbal itself (asking) followed by its direct object (questions).

3. If formed from the verb "be," a verbal noun can have a predicate noun or predicate adjective as part of its internal structure--

Mr. Wilson enjoyed being-an-inventor.

This package (being-an-inventor) is the direct object of the verb "enjoyed." However, its internal structure consists of the verbal (being) followed by its predicate noun (inventor).

His wife did not enjoy being-poor.

This package (being-poor) is the direct object of the verb "enjoy." Its internal structure consists of the verbal (being) + its predicate adjective (poor).

A verbal noun phrase can contain a negative—

Not-keeping-score was a mistake.

The whole package (not-keeping-score) is the subject of the sentence. Its internal structure consists of an adverb (not) + the verbal (keeping) + (score) the direct object of the verbal.

Usage Note--when a verbal noun phrase follows a preposition, it is the whole phase unit that is the object, not simply the word that follows the preposition.

Correct--The school has no record of (my-winning-the-poetry- prize).

Incorrect--The school has no record of (me-winning-the-poetry-prize).

At first glance, "me" seems to be the object of the preposition "of." However, if we enclose the entire verbal phrase in parentheses, we see that the word following the preposition is really part of the phrase. It modifies the verbal noun "winning" and therefore needs to be in the possessive case. The same is true if the word after the preposition is a noun instead of a pronoun. This noun is acting as an adjective and therefore should be in the possessive.

Correct--The school has no record of (Mary's-winning-the-poetry-prize).

Incorrect--The school has no record of (Mary-winning-the-poetry- prize).

46

In the following sentences, use hyphens to connect the words in the verbal noun package and enclose the package in parentheses. Then determine the noun job that the whole package is doing.
Example—

> Marie looked forward to (meeting-her-new-neighbor). "Meeting-her-new-neighbor" is the object of the preposition "to."

1. Alfred's hobby was repairing clocks.
2. Swimming laps in a pool is good exercise.
3. The restaurant owner liked trying foreign recipes.
4. My worst habit is buying new gadgets.
5. Waiting for the bus on a cold night is no fun.
6. My mother was surprised at my winning the contest.
7. The zoo signs prohibited feeding the animals.
8. Joe's proudest achievement last semester was not skipping any classes.
9. The committee was opposed to revealing the donor's name.
10. Not eating vegetables can affect a person's health.

Exercise 11

Open up each of the verbal noun packages in the sentences above and determine the internal structure.

Verbal Adjective Phrases

A Verbal Adjective Phrase (called "a participial phrase" in traditional grammar) is a package of words acting as a unit. It consists of a verb form ending in "-ing,"ed or "en" + either a modifier and/or a complement. That unit will be modifying a noun--a standard adjective job. However, it has more freedom than a simple adjective, which always stands immediately before its noun. A verbal adjective phrase can stand on either side of its noun.

> Waving-a-white-flag, the soldier leaped to the platform.
> The soldier, waving-a-white-flag, leaped to the platform.

In each case, the package is modifying the noun "soldier."

Punctuation note--When the verbal adjective phrase begins the sentence, as in the first sentence above, it is followed by a comma. This is a signal to the reader that the important part of the sentence--the subject--is coming next. When the verbal adjective phrase follows its noun--as in the second sentence above--it is set off at each end by commas to indicate that it is not essential to the sentence.

Usage Note--It is essential that the phrase be next to its noun in order to avoid the error known as a "dangling participle." This occurs when the phrase is standing next to the wrong noun or when the noun it modifies does not even appear in the sentence.

> Dangling---Hidden-in-her-pocket, the spy got away with the key.
> Correct--The spy got away with the key hidden-in-her-pocket.

"Hidden-in-her-pocket" is a verbal adjective phrase modifying "key."

> Dangling--Confused-by-my-questions, a recess was called.
> Correct--- The judge, confused-by-my-questions, called a recess.

Confused-by-my-questions" is a verbal adjective phrase modifying "judge."

Exercise 12

Hyphenate all verbal adjective phrases. Identify the noun or pronoun immediately before or after the phrase. If the phrase does not modify this noun or if there is no noun nearby, this is a dangling modifier. Rewrite the sentence to eliminate the error. Not every sentence contains an error. Any necessary commas have been omitted. Example—

> Dangling---Examining-a-footprint-of-the-fugitive a bear attacked the ranger.
> Correction--A bear attacked the ranger examining-a-footprint-of-the- fugitive.

1. Following the wrong trail hours were lost by the hikers.
2. Watching the greyhound races I forgot my dental appointment.
3. Crowded into a corner by autograph hunters my sympathies were with the famous singer.
4. Having swept through the village much damage was done by the storm.
5. Having introduced the speaker everyone saw the chairman leave the room.
6. Traced in ink our leader found the map easy to read.
7. The clown waved to the crowd seated on a soapbox.
8. Broken beyond repair the salesman regretted the loss of the vase.
9. Brought down by a single shot I picked up the bird.
10. Having been left on the pier the ferryboat sailed without us.

If it stands alone in a sentence and therefore is not a phrase, a verbal adjective must still be next to the noun it modifies--

The spy got away with the hidden key.

"Hidden" is still a verbal adjective modifying "key," but because it is a single word, not a phrase, it precedes the noun it modifies, as is customary in English.

Complications of the Verbal Adjective Phrase

The main ingredient of a verbal adjective phrase is not as easy to recognize as the main ingredient of a verbal noun phrase. All verbal nouns end in "-ing."

Verbal adjectives have more variety because they come in two tenses--present and past--and because some English verbs are irregular.

Present tense verbal adjective phrase--

Weeping-inconsolably, the child ran after her mother.

This looks like a verbal noun phrase until we see that it modifies the noun "child."

Past tense verbal adjective phrase----

Having-paid-my-hotel-bill, I went to the airport.

Since a pronoun can be a substitute for a noun, it can be modified by a verbal adjective. "Having-paid-my-hotel-bill" modifies the pronoun "I." The past tense verbal sometimes uses "having" plus the past participle of a verb, but sometimes it will simply use the past participle.

Painted-bright-red, Jim's car was conspicuous.

This verbal adjective phrase modifies the noun "car." The possessive "Jim's" is acting like a second adjective modifying "car." A possessive noun always acts like an adjective and always precedes its noun.

Having-painted-his-car-bright-red, Jim became well known.

This verbal adjective phrase modifies the noun "Jim."

Purchased-for-an-unknown-collector, the painting disappeared.

This verbal adjective phrase modifies the noun "painting."

Verbal Noun Phrase vs. Verbal Adjective Phrase

Both these phrases can look alike, but one will be acting like a noun while the other will be acting like an adjective.

Noun use--Wearing-a-warm-sweater is a good idea in winter.   (Subject of the verb)

Adjective use--Wearing-a-warm-sweater, Joe went for a walk. (modifies "Joe.")

Internal Structure of the Verbal Adjective Phrase

Since verbal adjectives have the DNA of verbs, they have some of the privileges of verbs even while they are doing an adjective job.

1. A verbal adjective can be modified by one or more adverbs-

> Singing-happily, the children marched down the street. (present tense)
>
> Having-sung-loudly, I woke up the family. (past tense)

2. A verbal adjective can take a direct object--

> Opening-my-package, the inspector frowned.
>
> Having reserved a room, Max hailed a taxi.

3. If formed from the verb "be," a verbal adjective can take a predicate noun—

> Being-club-treasurer, Jerry collected our dues.
>
> Having-been-club-treasurer, Mary knew which bills to pay.

4. If formed from the verb "be." a verbal adjective can take a predicate adjective--

> Being-popular, Tom was elected chairman.
>
> Having-been-popular-in-the-past, Fred was surprised by his defeat.

A verbal adjective phrase can be negative--

> Not-smiling-at-my-joke, Aunt Edna left the room.

Caution--A verb ending in "-ing" can be any one of three things. It can be a verbal noun, a verbal adjective, or part of the sentence verb in the progressive tense.

1. Verbal noun phrase--

> The-continual-barking kept us awake.

"Barking" is the verbal in the verbal noun phrase "the-continual-barking." It cannot be dropped from the sentence because the whole phrase is the subject of the sentence.

2. Verbal adjective phrase--

> Barking-loudly, the dog kept us awake.
>
> The dog, barking-loudly, kept us awake.
>
> The barking dog kept us awake.

"Barking-loudly" is a verbal adjective phrase modifying the noun "dog." "Barking" is a verbal adjective modifying "dog." These verbals can be dropped--like any other adjectives--without damaging the basic sentence structure--"The dog kept us awake." This proves that the "-ing" form is a verbal adjective.

If the -"ing" form is part of the main verb in the sentence, it is not a verbal adjective and it cannot be dropped. It is the essential part of the main verb combination and indicates that the verb is in the progressive tense, signifying continued action--"was barking."

> The dog was barking all night.

It can be reduced to the simple past--
The dog barked all night.
It cannot be dropped.
(The progressive tense, which indicates continued action, is formed by the appropriate form of the auxiliary "be" + the "-ing" form of the main verb. See Appendix A.)

Exercise 13

Hyphenate the words in the verbal noun phrases and verbal adjective phrases in the following sentences. In the case of noun phrases, indicate which noun job they are doing. In the case of adjective phrases, indicate which noun they modify.
Test each answer by trying to drop the phrase. (A verbal noun phrase cannot be dropped without damaging the basic sentence structure. A verbal adjective phrase can be dropped) Any necessary commas have been omitted.
Examples--The boy liked the excitement of-racing-old-cars.
"Racing-old-cars" is a verbal noun phrase acting as object of the preposition "of."
It cannot be dropped because a preposition must have an object.
The salesman smiling-warmly offered me a discount.
"Smiling-warmly" is a verbal adjective phrase modifying "salesman." It can be dropped--
The salesman offered me a discount.

1. Pitching a no-hit game in baseball is a great accomplishment.
2. The bank facing Broadway closed last week.
3. We watched a man digging in a nearby field.
4. The campers began gathering wood for a fire.
5. Seeing the danger instantly the ranger pulled me to one side.
6. He found the old letters after ransacking the desk drawers.
7. My missing the train was the result of a series of mishaps.
8. Wondering about the former owner of the house we explored the attic.
9. From our balcony we saw the flags blowing in the wind.
10. Becoming a fine pianist requires years of practice.

Infinitive Phrases

An Infinitive Phrase is another package of words acting as a unit. This unit is the most powerful of the three kinds of verbal phrases. It can act as a noun, as an adjective, or an adverb. It is also the easiest to recognize, as it is usually preceded by "to." Occasionally the phrase will be introduced by "for" and a subject word.
It is hard for Mary-to-learn-the cello.
If the subject word is a pronoun, it must be in the objective case--

It is hard for us-to-believe-his-story.

Usage Note--Split Infinitive--Traditionally It has been considered a writing error if any word is put between the "to" and its verb-- "to-boldly-go" instead of "to-go-boldly." However, modern writers do sometimes insert an adverb in cases where putting the adverb after the verb or before the "to" would sound awkward--

> awkward--to-never-smoke
> acceptable--never-to-smoke
> awkward--to-frequently-skip-lunch
> awkward--frequently-to-skip-lunch
> acceptable--to-skip-lunch-frequently

Infinitive phrase as noun--
> 1. Subject--To-travel-first-class is a luxury.
> 2. Direct object--Children usually hate to-do-homework.
> 3. Predicate noun--My ambition is to-become-an-artist.

Infinitive phrase as adjective-
> The mayor proposed a plan to-assist-the elderly.
> "To-assist-the-elderly" modifies the noun "plan."

Infinitive phrase as adverb--
> The police officer was ready to-use-force.
> "To-use-force" modifies the adjective "ready."

Internal Structure of Infinitive Phrases

Since infinitive phrases have the DNA of verbs, they have some of the privileges of verbs even when the whole unit is acting like a noun, an adjective, or an adverb--
1. The verb in the infinitive phrase can make use of the auxiliaries "have/having" and "be/being/been" to show tense or the passive.
> The explorers were reported to-have-found-the-treasure.
> The girls were supposed to-have-been-home-early.
> Mr. Smith seemed to-be-having-trouble-with-his-car.
> Bobby was accustomed to-being-first-on-line.
2. The verb can be modified by an adverb--
> To-save-regularly is sometimes difficult.
3. The verb can take a direct object--
> The prisoner was reluctant to-tell-his-real-name.
> ("His real name" is the direct object of "tell.")
4. If formed with the linking verb "be," that verb can take a predicate noun or predicate adjective—
> The missing man was known to-have-been-a-doctor.

("Doctor" is the predicate noun after the verb "been.")
Teachers are expected to-be-resourceful.
("Resourceful" is the predicate adjective after the verb "be.")
Infinitive phrases can also be made negative—
Harry decided not-to-buy-a-puppy.

Exercise 14

In the following sentences, enclose the infinitive phrases in parentheses and explain their use as noun, adjective, or adverb.
Example—
The engine of the car began (to-make-a-strange-noise).
Noun-- direct object of verb "began."
1. Walter Brown's ambition was to win the mayoral election.
2. To learn Latin would be a hard task for young Tommy.
3. The tourists were anxious to visit the palace.
4. The purpose of the lesson was to teach the value of patience.
5. The detective's plan to trap the criminal was successful.
6. The engineer did not expect to take a long vacation.
7. The motto of the college has always been "To Advance Knowledge."
8. My mother told me not to tease the dog.
9. To have my own credit card would be a great convenience.
10. For a long time the boys had been trying to build a rocket.

Exercise 15

Describe the internal structure of the infinitive phrases in the sentences above.
Example—
After a while the train began (to-skip-some-stations).
Infinitive "to skip" + direct object "some stations"

Exercise 16

Hyphenate and label all verbal phrases in the following sentences and decide how each is being used--as noun, adjective, or adverb. Any necessary commas have been omitted.
Example—
Leaving a trail of breadcrumbs the children walked through the forest.
"Leaving-a-trail-of-breadcrumbs" is a verbal adjective phrase that modifies the noun "children."
1. Displaying his splendid tail the peacock waited for me to feed him.

2. We had hoped to catch an early train but waiting for the taxi kept us from getting to the station on time.
3. The woman asked the tailor to shorten her coat because she didn't want to look dowdy.
4. Crabgrass growing vigorously was taking over the lawn.
5. Hanging pictures in a new apartment proved to be a test of my patience.
6. Jane was enthusiastic about doing the crossword puzzle.
7. The old woman refused to be evacuated by the rescue crew.
8. Flying a kite never seemed easy to me.
9. Having planned the expedition carefully Foster expected no problems.
10. Nobody was ready to interrupt the man telling a long and tiresome story.

Embedding

Any kind of phrase in an English sentence can be embedded in a larger phrase, and it is possible to have single, double, and triple embedding, as we'll see in coming chapters. Our interest at this point is to note the embedding of verbal phrases.

> After the storm we were told to avoid walking on the beach.

Stripping the sentence down to basics and taking it in steps may make it more clear--

> We were told (something)--basic sentence
> to avoid (something)--infinitive phrase object of "told"
> walking on the beach--noun phrase object of "avoid".

> Hoping to overcome the decline of his popularity the rock star began to tour the country.

> star began (something)--basic sentence
> to tour the country--infinitive phrase object of "began"
> hoping (something)--verbal adjective phrase modifying "star"
> to overcome the decline of his popularity--infinitive phrase object of "hoping"

("The" and "rock" are separate modifiers of the noun "star" and are not relevant to our analysis of verbal phrases.)

Third Word Package--Pair/Series

The third kind of word package is easy to recognize--

Red-and-green are complementary colors.

Red-yellow-and-blue are primary colors.

In the first sentence we have a Pair of words forming a package which is the subject of the sentence. In the second sentence we have a Series of words forming a package which is the subject of the sentence. A series can consist of any number of words, but it is usual to limit them to three unless we are making a list as in the following sentence—

The most popular desserts are ice-cream-cake-sherbet-pie-pudding-and-fruit.

This series is correct, but we are straining the reader's patience. Three is the best number to keep in mind whether we are listing reasons, giving examples, or suggesting possibilities. Four is overdoing it, and two seems stingy.

Punctuation note--the words in a series are separated by commas.

The most popular desserts are ice cream, cake, sherbet, pie, pudding, and fruit.

A comma is never used with a pair.

The items in a pair can be linked by "and, or, nor, &, but"--the coordinate conjunctions used to connect grammatically equal items. (The connector "&" is not used in formal writing.)

We can go by car-or-plane.

The tortoise in the famous race was slow-but-sure.

The queen liked neither roses-nor-lilies.

I will choose either France-or-Italy for my vacation.

Both diamonds-and-emeralds are expensive.

"Either" works in tandem with "or" and "neither" works in tandem with "nor." "Both" is used with "and."

In a series we have the choice of using the connectors above or of using just commas, or of using a combination of conjunction and comma. Our choice depends upon the effect we want the sentence to have--

Red and yellow and blue are primary colors.

Red, yellow, blue are primary colors.

Red, yellow, and blue are primary colors.

The repetition of "and" slows the sentence down. The use of just commas creates an abruptness that is generally undesirable. The combination of comma with "and" is the usual choice.

Punctuation note--The use of the comma preceding "and" in the last sentence above is a choice some writers prefer and others do not. The sentence is correct either way.

The more important punctuation question is whether or not to put a comma after the last item in a series. The answer is definitely not. The commas, if any, belong inside the series, not outside, for in many cases we would be putting a comma between the subject and the verb. This we never do.

Incorrect--Red, yellow, and blue, are primary colors.
The series is a package working as the subject of the verb and must not be separated from the verb by any punctuation mark.

Coordination

Items with similar grammatical value must be used in a pair or series. The items may be single nouns, verbs, adjectives, or adverbs or they may be packages such as phrases. We can even have a pair or series of little sentences in one big supersentence. The connectors--"and, but, or, nor"--demand equality. This is called Coordination.

Examples--
Joseph-and-William are soccer players. --a pair of nouns as a subject package
The performer sang-danced-and-told jokes. --a series of verbs with one subject
The newcomer was ready to-stay-here-or-to-go-away --a pair of infinitive phrases as a package modifying the adjective "ready"
We drove across-the-river-but-not-into-the-woods. --a pair of prepositional phrases as a package modifying the verb "drove." The negative "not" has no effect on the grammatical structure.

Incorrect because unequal grammatical value—
Watching-TV-and-chocolate are my favorites.--a verbal noun phrase and a simple noun cannot be joined by a coordinating conjunction.

Exercise 17

Locate every pair and series. What does each consist of? What grammatical job in the sentence is each one doing? Any necessary commas have been omitted.

1. Four or five hikers stopped in Harry's diner for coffee doughnuts and gossip.
2. The furnace shut down a water pipe broke the dog ran away and the cook went to bed with a headache.
3. You should not pick wildflowers be careless with matches or forget about bears if you want to live outdoors in safety and in harmony with nature.

4. My choice of blue satin and lace bridesmaid's dresses pleased neither Gertrude nor Eliza.
5. The theaters restaurants and museums of New York City interested Don but bored his mother and father.

Fourth Word Package--Clusters

Although it is widely used in English sentences, the Cluster as a structure or word package has never been discussed in traditional grammar. A cluster--unlike a phrase, which always has two essential elements--is a group of words with only one essential element known as the Head Word.

Phrase--preposition + noun or pronoun object
      verbal + complement (object or predicate noun) and/or modifier
Cluster--a head word (noun, verb, adjective, or adverb) + complement (object or predicate noun) and/or modifier
Since a cluster is a package it is used as a unit, and like all other packages, it can contain smaller packages (embedding).

For example --
      in school--a phrase consisting of two essential elements (preposition + noun object)
      flying a plane--a phrase consisting of two essential elements (verbal noun and its object)
      a little red beetle--a cluster that can be stripped down to just its head word "beetle"
      had been laughing loudly--a cluster that can be stripped down to its head word "laughing"

The head word of a cluster can be a noun, verb, adjective or adverb with any number of modifiers. Since a cluster is a package used as a unit, it can contain smaller packages (embedding).

Adjective and Adverb Clusters

Adjective and adverb clusters are less common than noun and verb clusters, and they are the easiest to identify.

Examples of adjective clusters--
1. quite expensive--adverbial modifier +adjective (the head word)
2. not very warm--negator + adverbial modifier + adjective (the head word)
3. cold as ice--adjective (head word) + adverbial modifier (prepositional phrase)

4. more expensive than we had ordered--adjective (head word) +
    dependent clause acting as adverbial modifier
(A dependent clause is a major league package and will be discussed
in the next chapter. "More expensive" is the comparative form of the
adjective "expensive." (See Appendix A.)

Examples of adverb clusters--
1. not too awkwardly--negator + adverbial modifier + adverb (head
    word)
2. rather cautiously--adverbial modifier + adverb (head word)
3. more slowly as the music faded--adverb(head word) in comparative
    form (See Appendix A) + modifying dependent clause.
4. sooner than the audience expected--adverb (head word) + modifying
    dependent clause

Exercise 18

Find and label all adjective and adverb clusters. How is each used?
Underline the head word in each. (Any necessary commas have been
omitted.)

1. Not very truthfully the culprit maintained that he was totally honest.
2. A rather grumpy clerk stared at the newcomers and announced in
    barely audible tones that their reservations most obviously had
    been lost.
3. The girl looked fresh as a daisy and seemed happy as a lark while
    she unwrapped the really gaudy boxes.
4. More slowly than usual the bright little boy walked his sister across
    the extremely snowy playground.
5. The too eager new waiter handed me the menu quite dramatically.

Noun Clusters

We often find that some or all of the nouns in a sentence have
modifiers both to their right and to their left. This is due to the fact that
one-word modifiers of the noun go before it and package modifiers of
the noun (phrases, clusters, and clauses) go to its right. The noun itself
will be doing one of its important grammatical jobs--acting as subject
(N-1), indirect object (N-2), direct object(N-3) predicate noun (Nn-1),
objective complement (Nn-3), or it will be doing its least important job--
object of a preposition.

The one-word modifiers of a noun can be one or several kinds--
determiner, demonstrative, possessive noun or pronoun, quantifier,

negator, or adjective. (See Chapter 2.) There can be only one of each of these except for adjectives.

A noun can be preceded by one, two or even three adjectives--
        "Mrs. Brown's shabby old house."
(Remember that adding an apostrophe + "-s" to a noun to form a possessive actually turns that noun into an adjective.)

Writing note--Good writers try to limit their use of adjectives.

The noun with its modifiers is a package known as a noun cluster. The noun is called the Head Word--
        a boat
        the new boat
        six old boats
        that boat drifting on the river
        no boat ever designed
        our boat in the weekly race
        John's new boat that he soon gave to his brother

Sometimes we find a way to telescope the post-noun package into a single word which is then allowed to precede the noun. Frequently this is done by use of a hyphen which joins the words into a single unit-
        "paint-smeared fingers" instead of "fingers smeared with
        paint".
Both of these are noun clusters with "fingers" as the head word.
        "high-priced cars" instead of "cars with a high price."
The head word in each of these noun clusters is "cars."

Writing note--It is not advisable to use this hyphen device very often because it can become a distraction for the reader, who is expecting the more common post-noun modifier.

Noun clusters can occur anywhere in a sentence. They can be short or long--
        My-cat has a-habit-of-drinking-from-a-running-tap-in-the-
        kitchen.
"My-cat" is a short noun cluster (head word is "cat") and "a-habit-of-drinking-from-a-running-tap-in-the-kitchen" is a long noun cluster (head word is "habit") which contains a smaller noun cluster--"a-running-tap-in-the-kitchen" (head word is "tap") which contains a smaller noun cluster "the-kitchen" (head word is "kitchen.")

In its use of noun modifiers, English shows a tendency to imitate its cousin language, German. German likes to string nouns together like freight cars without using visible connectors. For example,

Dreiviertelstunde (three-quarters of an hour) is written as one word made up of three--*drei*-three, *viertel*- fourth, *stunde*-hour. English doesn't go as far as German does, although we can find some cases where two nouns were joined to make one word, such as "beehive" and "teacup" instead of "bees' hive" and "tea cup" ("cup for tea"). There does not seem to be any rule for this. After all, in the case of "coffee cup," we still have two separate words. Hyphens that were sometimes used to join two words into one are beginning to disappear. Only a modern dictionary can tell us whether two words that now make one noun have been simply jammed together or are joined by a hyphen, or are still written separately--"birdbath, bird-watcher, car wash." Even the comparatively new word "e-mail" has begun appearing as "email."

Nowadays when a word has both an adjectival and a noun form, we often choose the noun form (which is usually shorter) to do the work of an adjective. It is then called a noun adjunct. (See Chapter 2.) For example, we see "recreation activities" instead of "recreational activities" and "wool jacket" instead of "woolen jacket."
There is also a modern tendency to drop the genitive (the "of" phrase), so that, for example, "a tale of winter" becomes "a winter's tale" or even "a winter tale."
The abandonment of adjectival forms in favor of noun adjuncts reflects our preference for speed. Another aspect of this preference is the modern use of shortened words in informal speech and writing-- "delicatessen" becomes "deli," "laboratory" becomes "lab," and "gymnasium" becomes "gym."

Embedding--one noun cluster can be embedded in others which are often found in prepositional phrases.
> The founder of the famous university in my town was a man with an interest in young people.

Noun clusters--
> The founder of the famous university in my town-- head word is "founder" This cluster is the subject of the sentence.
> the famous university in my town--head word "university" This cluster is the object of the preposition ""of."
> my town--head word is "town." This cluster is the object of the preposition "in."

Exercise 19

Find every noun cluster and underline the head word. How is each cluster used?
Method--look for nouns and then see if they have modifiers.

1. It was midnight when an iceberg struck the cargo ship.
2. A Florida beach is our favorite winter destination.
3. The old man living by the lake went to see why his dog was barking.
4. In the shop window one blue bottle caught the afternoon sunlight.
5. The stranded party boat drew curious glances from the passing ferry.
6. This necklace inherited from my grandmother is very valuable.
7. A young man with a shaved head was the manager of the hair salon.
8. Maria's new admirer sent her one dozen long-stemmed roses.
9. The steamship company had said that the Titanic was the safest ship afloat.
10. The boy with the lollipop in one hand wanted to hold my frisky little puppy with the other.

Verb Clusters

Verb clusters occur in all but the shortest sentences. If we cross out the subject, what is left is bound to be a verb cluster unless it consists of just one word.

> The big dog growled.

If we cross out the subject, we just have "growled." That cannot be a verb cluster because it is single word.

> The big dog growled menacingly.

If we cross out the subject, we have "growled menacingly," a verb cluster whose head word is "growled." (head word + adverb modifier)

> The deliveryman dropped all his packages.

If we cross out the subject, we have "dropped all his packages" with "dropped" as the head word. (head word + a noun cluster acting as direct object)

> My uncle has given me a wristwatch.

If we cross out the subject, we have a verb cluster whose head word is "given."

(auxiliary "has" + head word + indirect object + direct object)

> The smell of fresh paint in our guest room could have caused little Peter's headache.

If we cross out the subject, we have a verb cluster whose head word is "caused."

(modal + auxiliary + head word + noun cluster as direct object.)

> The cause of the explosion was a broken gas pipe.

If we cross out the subject, we have a verb cluster with the head word "was."

(head word + noun cluster acting as predicate noun.)

> The cause of the explosion was not a broken gas pipe.

As these examples demonstrate, a verb cluster can consist of just two words or many words--negator, modals, auxiliaries, complements, and modifiers.

Embedding--A verb cluster can be embedded in a noun cluster just as a noun cluster can be embedded in a verb cluster. Adjective and adverb clusters can turn up anywhere.

Exercise 20

Find each verb cluster and underline the head word. Label the other words or structures in the cluster.
Example--My sister found the library book (which) I had been seeking for several days.
There are two verb clusters here, one inside the other--
> a) found the library book (which) I had been seeking for several days
>   head word-"found" + a noun cluster
> b) had been seeking for several days
>   auxiliary "had" + auxiliary "been" + head word "seeking" + prepositional phrase.

1. The fish swallowed the bait on my hook.
2. You must have noticed the tulip display.
3. The little boy could never remember his teacher's name.
4. The school Christmas pageant has been a tradition for many years.
5. My neighbor's dog barked at my visitors.
6. Roger crossed the street as the bus came around the corner.
7. Alaskan guides always tell hikers to beware of the bears.
8. Melting glaciers are a concern of many towns and villages relying upon them for a municipal water supply.
9. Sudden thunderstorms did not bring enough rain to the little prairie town that was suffering a drought.
10. Butterflies have been disappearing from people's gardens in the last few years.

Exercise 21

Locate and label all clusters--noun, verb, adjective, adverb. Underline the head word in each.
Example--The-usually-calm-waters-of-the-bay were growing very-rough in-the-violent-storm.
> the usually calm waters of the bay--noun cluster, head word "waters"
> usually calm--adjective cluster, head word "calm"
> the bay--noun cluster, head word "bay"

were growing very rough in the violent storm--verb
cluster, head word "growing"
very rough--adjective cluster, head word "rough"
the violent storm--noun cluster, head word "storm"

1. The very rich people in the summer cottages almost always stayed on the beach until dusk.
2. The rather simple task of building a model igloo will be completed in a few weeks.
3. Very generously the owner of the motorboat lent it to the local Boy Scouts.
4. Every daffodil along the garden path had disappeared quite mysteriously.
5. Only really expert divers in wetsuits should be looking for treasure in that sunken ship.

CHAPTER 4

MAJOR LEAGUE WORD PACKAGES
Independent and Dependent Clauses
Grammatical Equality and Inequality
Connectors

We have seen how minor-league word packages (phrase, pair/series, and cluster) can be buried in sentences and often, though not always, dropped. Much descriptive detail is supplied by minor-league packages like prepositional phrases and adjective verbal phrases which are not necessary elements of the sentence pattern. Now we come to the major-league word package that can never be dropped. This word package is known as a clause.

A clause is another name for a sentence pattern. When it stands alone we call it a simple sentence. When we combine it with another sentence pattern, we call it a clause. Whatever its name, it is the most important of all the grammatical structures. When we combine two or more clauses, we create a supersentence.

Combining clauses into supersentences helps us avoid the monotony of a series of simple short sentences. More important, a careful choice of connectives serves to show how the two or more ideas in our supersentence are related.
Are the ideas in, say, two combined clauses equal to each other or is one less important? Do we want to show a cause-and-effect relationship? Do we want to make a statement accompanied by a concession? Is there a time relationship to be indicated? Does one of the clauses add description or explanation?

Sometimes when we combine two clauses, we indicate that the ideas expressed in each clause are of equal importance. At other times we make sure that the idea in one clause is less important than the other. This is done by using a connecting word which will produce the effect we seek.
If two clauses are joined into one sentence without a connector, the result is a Run-on Sentence, which is a writing error.

Supersentences often have more than two combined clauses. However, in this chapter we will limit ourselves to the simplest supersentences--those with just two combined clauses.

The connecting words fall into various groups known as coordinate conjunctions, subordinate conjunctions, relative pronouns, relative adjective, relative adverbs, and interrogators. It is also possible to connect two independent clauses with nothing more than a semicolon.

> The airport waiting area was crowded; the plane was late.
>
> N-1 link verb + adj ; N-1 + link verb + adj

This punctuation connector should be used sparingly. Overuse will give sentences an abruptness than is not pleasing to the reader.

Grammatical Equality

One kind of connecting word ("and, but, or, nor") creates a balance showing that the ideas in each clause are equally important. These connectors are called Coordinate Conjunctions. The sentence patterns in each of the clauses should be generally similar. Reversing the order of the two statements often makes no difference. It is the connector that creates the balance. However, we sometimes have to juggle a word or two for semantic reasons

> 1a) I am studying French and my sister is studying German.
>
> N-1 + action verb + N-3 and N-1 + action verb + N-3
>
> 1b) My sister is studying German and I am studying French.
>
> N-1 + action verb + N-3   and N-1 + action verb + N-3
>
> 2a) I am studying French but my sister is studying German.
>
> N-1 + action verb + N-3 but N-1 + action verb + N-3
>
> 2b) My sister is studying German but I am studying French.
>
> N-1 + action verb + N-3 but N-1 + action verb + N-3

The semantic personality of the connector "but" adds something to the balance between the two ideas. It highlights the contrast.

> 3a) Joe will have to get a job or his wife will have to get one.
>
> N-1 + action verb + N-3 or N-1 + action verb + N-3
>
> 3b) Joe's wife will have to get a job or he will have to get one.
>
> N-1+ action verb + N-3 or N-1 + action verb + N-3

Both clauses are equal, but the connector "or" highlights the notion of alternative actions. (Notice the readjustment of the pronouns.)

3c) Either Joe will have to get a job or his wife will have
to get one.

N-1 + action verb + N-3 or N-1 + action verb + N-3

The addition of "either" as a partner with "or" is optional. It is used to
highlight the idea of choice.

4a) complications of the negative--.Dad does not like jazz
nor does he like rock music.

Dad does not like jazz

N-1 + "do" + "not" + action verb + N-3

+ negator connector "nor"

does he like rock music

"do" + N-1 + action verb + N-3

The reversal of "he" and "does" is caused by a semantic quirk
generated by the use of the negative "nor." This reversal problem does
not arise often because we do not use "nor" very much. It sounds too
literary for everyday English.

Dad does not like jazz

+ and

he does not like rock music.

N-1 + "do" + "not" + action verb + N-3

Putting the negative coloring in "not" rather than in the connector
("nor") makes it possible to use normal word order.

The average American would write the sentence as "Dad does not like
jazz or rock." N-1 + "do" + "not" + action verb + N-3 + connector + N-3
This connector is joining two N-3s in order to form a construction
known as a Pair. (See Chapter 3.)

When three or more clauses are combined into one supersentence, at
least one of them will be unequal. A supersentence with more than two
equally connected clauses is unusual

Semicolon as connector--

Mary plays the piano ; Ellen plays the violin.

N-1 action verb + N-3 ; N-1 + action verb + N-3

Mary plays the piano but Ellen plays the violin.

N-1 + action verb + N-3 but N-1 + action verb + N-3

You take the high road; I'll take the low road.

N-1 + action verb + N-3 ; N-1 + action verb + N-3

You take the high road and I'll take the low road.

N-1 + action verb + N-3 and N-1 + action verb + N-3

The clauses in these two sentences will accept the semicolon as a
connector in place of "but" and "and."

Caution-- The presence of a coordinate conjunction in a sentence does
not guarantee that the sentence consists of two equal clauses. It might
be a simple sentence (one clause) containing a pair or a series.

Lightning struck the house, but it spared the barn.

N-1 + action verb + N-3 but N-1 + action verb + N-3

This is a supersentence sentence containing two independent clauses. The coordinate conjunction is followed by a subject (N-1) and a second verb.

Lightning struck the house but spared the barn.

N-1 + action verb + N-3 but action verb + N-3.

Since there is no N-1 after the conjunction, we do not have a second clause.

Lightning struck the house and the barn.

N-1 + action verb + N-3 and N-3

This is a simple sentence with one clause which has a pair of direct objects.

A supersentence with two independent clauses must have a subject (N-1) following the conjunction and preceding the second verb . N-1 + verb...conjunction N-1 + verb...

Two clauses--The old man was a retired sheriff and his son was the police chief,

N-1 + link verb + Nn-1 and N-1 + link verb + Nn-1

One clause with a pair as predicate noun-- The old man was a retired sheriff and a former police chief,

N-1 + link verb + Nn-1 and Nn-1

The old man and his son were enthusiastic fishermen.

N-1 and N-1 + link verb + Nn-1

Here we have a simple sentence with one clause which has a pair as subject.

Grammatical Inequality

Sometimes when we are constructing a supersentence, we want to show that the two (or three) ideas are not of equal importance. We make one of the clauses subordinate to the other simply by our choice of the connector. Just as adding water to coffee will weaken it, so adding a subordinating connector will weaken the clause it introduces. Then we add this weakened clause (subordinate) to an independent clause to make a supersentence. (The terms "subordinate" and "dependent" are used interchangeably.)

Subordinate Conjunctions

The connectors that weaken a clause and attach it to an independent clause are called Subordinate Conjunctions. This group includes the following--

"after, although, as, as if, because, before, if, since, that, though, till, until, unless, whether, while." These connectors create subordinate (dependent) clauses which can never stand alone.

Caution--Some of these connectors look exactly like other words that do a different grammatical job. Examples of these look-alike words can be found in Chapter 5.

The making of a supersentence with a subordinate clause----
New York is a large city.--independent clause
Because New York is a large city--the clause is no longer independent. It must now be combined with an independent clause. If it is used alone, it becomes a Sentence Fragment.
New York offers many business opportunities--new independent clause to be combined.
Because New York is a large city, it offers many business opportunities--supersentence
Because N-1 + link verb + Nn-1, N-1 + action verb + N-3
alternate version--New York offers many business opportunities because it is a large city.
N-1 + action verb + N-3 because N-1 + link verb + Nn-1
Notice the use of the pronoun "it" to avoid repeating "New York."

The writer can choose to put the subordinate clause first or second. Both supersentences are grammatically correct. We would logically expect the connector "because" to occur between the two clauses as the coordinate conjunctions do. That cannot happen because a subordinate conjunction must head the less important clause even when that clause comes first.

While all of the subordinate conjunctions do the same connecting job, each one has a different meaning that affects the meaning of the whole supersentence.

Independent clause + Dependent clause = Supersentence
1. I will buy a new sailboat after I save enough money.--time relationship
   N-1 + action verb + N-3 after N-1 + action verb + N-3
2. I will buy a new sailboat although I can't afford it.—concession
   although N-1 action verb N-3
3. I will buy a new sailboat as I want to enjoy my vacation.—cause
   as N-1 action verb + N-3
4. I will spend money as if I had a good job.--manner
   as if N-1 + action verb + N-3
5. I will buy a new sailboat before I get old.--time
   before N-1 + link verb + adj ("get" is a colloquial word for "become."
6. I will buy a new sailboat because I want it.--cause
   because N-1 + action verb + N-3
7. I will buy a new sailboat if I don't lose my job.--condition

if N-1 + action verb + N-3

8. I'm going to buy a new sailboat since my old one leaks.--cause
   since N-1 + action verb

9. My brother told me that I should not spend so much money.--specific
   N-1 action verb + N-2 + N-3
   that N-1 + action verb + N-3

10. I will buy a new sailboat though I can't afford it.--concession
    though N-1 + action verb + N-3

11. I will sail my new boat till I'm old.--time
    till N-1 + link verb ("I'm" is "I am") + adj

12. I will sail my new boat until I can afford a bigger one.--time
    until N-1 + action verb + N-3

13. I will buy a new sailboat unless I lose my job.--condition
    unless N-1 + action verb + N-3

14. I will buy a new sailboat whether (or not) you will lend me some
    money--choice
    whether (or not) N-1 + action verb + N-3

15. I will buy a new sailboat while I'm still young enough to enjoy it.--
    time
    while N-1 link verb + adj

It is grammatically possible to reverse the order of the clauses in almost all of the above sentences. However, because of quirks in word meanings, reversal of the order in sentences 3, 4, 9, 11, and 12 would not produce usable sentences.

Word meaning (semantics) is the outer layer of all grammatical structures--like a coat of paint--and it is not as precise and predictable as numbers in mathematics. Therefore certain word combinations will work very well together and others simply will not work together. Hence reversal of the clause sequence in sentences 3, 4, 11, and 12 will not produce usable sentences. Reversal in supersentence 9 is also impossible because it would produce a non-idiomatic statement. The dependent clause is acting as the direct object of the main verb "told" and therefore must retain its place in the sequence N-1 + verb + N-2 + N-3 "brother told me (something)".

All the other sentences have alternate versions--

1. After I save enough money, I'm going to buy a new sailboat.
2. Although I can't afford it, I'm going to buy a new sailboat.
5. Before I get old, I'm going to buy a new sailboat.
6. Because I want it, I'm going to buy a new sailboat.
7. If I don't lose my job, I'm going to buy a new sailboat.
8. Since my old sailboat leaks, I'm going to buy a new one.
   (Notice the shift in "sailboat" and the indefinite pronoun "one.")
9. Though I can't afford it, I'm going to buy a new sailboat.
10. Unless I lose my job, I'm going to buy a new sailboat.

11. Whether (or not) you lend me some money, I'm going to buy a new sailboat.
12. While I'm still young enough to enjoy it, I'm going to buy a new sailboat.

Punctuation note--When a verb construction such as a dependent clause precedes the main (independent) clause, that verb construction is followed by a comma. This is a signal to the reader that the main message of the sentence is coming .

One more subordinate conjunction ("than") requires special attention. It is used when the sentence is making a comparison, and it usually causes what is called an elliptical sentence--a sentence in which the second clause has an invisible verb. We say the invisible verb is understood because it would simply repeat the verb that appears in the first part of the sentence.

> Helen's little brother can skate better than she can (skate).
> N-1 + action verb than N-1 + (action verb)

Notice that the auxiliary "can" is repeated but the verb is understood. In these elliptical sentences, the adjective or adverb will be in the comparative form. (adverb "better.")
(See Comparison of Adjectives and Adverbs in Appendix A.)

> Mr. Smith will retire sooner than I will (retire). (adverb "sooner")
> N-1 +action verb than N-1 + (action verb)

Again the auxiliary is repeated ("will") but the verb is not repeated.
Two versions are possible when the verb is "be".--

> Mary is older than her brother (is old). (adjective "older")
> N-1 + link verb + adj than N-1 + (link verb + adj)
> Mary is older than her brother is (old).

Notice that with the verb "be" no auxiliary is used and the verb "be" can either be repeated or omitted.

With verbs other than "be," if there is no auxiliary to repeat, we supply one--"do."

> My friend likes winter better than I do (like winter.) (adverb "better")
> I like summer more than she does (like summer). (adverb "more")
> Helen's little brother skated better than she did (skate).
> Mr. Smith retired sooner than I did (retire). (adverb "sooner")

Elliptical clauses containing pronouns are often written incorrectly because of confusion about the case of the pronoun.

William always walks faster than me.--incorrect
The pronoun "me" is in the wrong case because in the understood part
of the elliptical clause, it is the subject.
William always walks faster than I (walk).--correct
N-1 + action verb than N-1 + (action verb)
Alternate correct version--William always walks faster than I do.
In this version, we have substituted the auxiliary "do" for the
understood verb "walk."
Sometimes the pronoun in the elliptical clause is the direct object, and
then it should be in the objective case—
The teacher helps Mary more than me (more than she
helps me)—correct
N-1 + action verb + N-3 than N-1 + (action verb) + N-3

The choice of the correct case of the pronoun can always be
determined by supplying the understood part of the elliptical clause.

Two-Job Connectors
Relators and Interrogators

We have seen how coordinate conjunctions and subordinate
conjunctions connect clauses in order to create supersentences.
Another group of connectors joins clauses but also does a second
grammatical job at the same time. These are called Relators (words
that relate --connect--two clauses) and Interrogators.
The Relators act as pronouns, adjectives, or adverbs at the same time
that they connect, and Interrogators turn the clauses they are
connecting into a question instead of a supersentence statement.
Relators and Interrogators must be placed at the beginning of their
clause regardless of the normal position they would occupy. (We saw
this happen with the positioning of subordinate conjunctions.)

Relative Pronouns
(that, which, who/whom)

Caution--"That," listed previously as a subordinate conjunction, now
turns out to have a twin working as a relative pronoun. It will occupy a
noun position--usually as subject or object of the verb.
Joe is the friend that taught me to drive. N-1 link verb +
Nn-1 that-N-1 + N-3
"That" is doing 2 jobs--connector + subject of "taught")
Process-
Independent clause--Joe is the friend.
Clause to be connected--The friend taught me to drive.
This becomes the dependent clause when we drop the second "the
friend" and replace it with the relative pronoun "that" --that taught me to

drive. We can put these together because "that" is also working as a connector. Since it is in the subject position, it is already at the beginning of the dependent clause where it is required to be..

This is the key that I found. (2 jobs--connector + object of "found")

N-1 + link verb + Nn-1 fhat-N-3 + N-1 + action verb

Process--

Independent clause--This is the key

Clause to be connected--I found the key

This becomes the dependent clause when we drop the second "the key" and replace it with "that"-- I found that

We must now move "that" to the beginning of the clause where it can do its second job, that of connecting --that I found--even though it is also working as object of the verb "found."

Caution--The relative pronoun "which" can replace "that" in the "key" sentence but cannot replace "that" in the sentence about Joe.

Correct--This the key which I found.

N-1 + link verb + Nn-1 which-N-3 + N-1 + action verb

Incorrect--Joe is the friend which taught me to drive.

"Which" can be used only when referring to things. In order to refer to persons, we must use "who/whom." "That" can refer to either things or persons.

Joe is the friend who taught me to drive. (2 jobs-- connector + subject of "taught") N-1 + link verb + who-N-1 + action verb + N-3

Process--

Independent clause--Joe is the friend.

Clause to be connected--The friend taught me to drive.

This becomes the dependent clause when we drop the second "the friend" and replace it with "who."--who taught me to drive.

Since "who" is the subject of "taught," it is already at the beginning of the dependent clause and need not be moved.

Joe is a person whom I admire. (2 jobs--connector + object of "admire")

N-1 + link verb+ Nn-1 whom-N-3 + N-1 + action verb

Process--

Independent clause--Joe is a person.

Clause to be connected--I admire a person.

This becomes a dependent clause when we drop the second "a person" and replace it with "whom"--I admire whom (The object form for "who" is "whom.")

We must now move "whom" to the beginning of the dependent clause where it can do its second job, that of connecting, even though it is also working as object of the verb "admire"--whom I admire

Note--If we use "that" as the connector instead of "who/whom," we do not have the problem of using the correct form. Furthermore, modern spoken English now tends to drop the connector altogether when it is acting as object of the verb--

> This is the key I found.   N-1 link verb + Nn-1 (that) N-1 + action verb
>
> Joe is a person I admire. N-1 + link verb + Nn-1 (whom) N-1 + action verb

Whether or not the connector is used in written English depends upon the degree of formality the writer wishes to project. The contemporary trend toward more speed and informality foreshadows the eventual total disappearance of this kind of connector.

Relative Adjective
(whose)

The relative adjective "whose," when spoken, sounds exactly like "who's," but they are entirely different words. "Whose" is the possessive form of "who." It always acts as a possessive adjective. However, because it is the possessive form of a pronoun and not of a noun, it does not have an apostrophe.

(Reminder--the possessive form of an noun is always marked by apostrophe +"-s" as in "John's." Even possessive pronouns that end in "s," such as "his, hers, its, ours, theirs" are never spelled with an apostrophe.)

The apostrophe in "who's" represents a different use of an apostrophe. It marks the omission of a letter in order to form a contraction. In this case, it is the "i" in "is" that is omitted. "Who is" becomes "who's." It has nothing to do with possessives.

"Whose" works as a relative adjective because it modifies a noun and at the same time connects a dependent clause with a main clause.

> Mr. Brown is the man whose horse won the first race.
>
> N-1 + link verb + Nn-1 (whose) N-1 + action verb + N-3

Process--

> Independent clause--Mr. Brown is the man.
>
> Clause to be connected-- horse won the first race.

We need a word to connect the two clauses and also a word to indicate Mr. Brown's ownership. "Whose" does both jobs.

"Whose" is the only relative adjective.

Relative Adverbs
(where, when, why, how, how often, how much)

I don't know where my wife put the key.
N-1 action verb (where) N-1 + action verb + N-3.
Process--
Independent clause--I don't know (something)
Clause to be connected--my wife put the key where
"Something" is an understood placeholder.
"Where" is an adverb modifying "put." It is also acting as the connector
of the two clauses and for this reason it must be moved to the
beginning of the inserted clause.
My wife put the key where
where my wife put the key
Now this clause is in order and can be inserted into the main clause in
place of the understood "something."

The curtain goes up when the play begins.
N-1 + action verb (when) N-1 + action verb
Process--
Independent clause--the curtain goes up
Clause to be connected--the play begins when
"When" is an adverb modifying "begins." We move it to the beginning
of its clause and then make the connection to the independent clause.

The mechanic knew why the car had stalled.
N-1 + action verb (why) N-1 + action verb
Process--
Independent clause--The mechanic knew (something)
Clause to be connected--the car had stalled why
Move the adverb "why" to the beginning of its clause--why the car had
stalled. Connect the two clauses.

I discovered how the cat found the mouse.
N-1 + action verb (how) N-1 + action verb +N-3
Process--
Independent clause--i discovered (something)
Clause to be connected--the cat found the mouse how
Move the adverb "how" to the beginning of the clause--how the cat
found the mouse. Connect the two clauses.

George told Maria how much he had spent on repairs.
("How much" acts as a single-word adverb)
N-1 + action verb + N-3 (how much N-1 + action verb

Process--
> Independent clause--George told Maria (something)
> Clause to be connected--he had spent how much on repairs

Move the adverb "how much" to the beginning of its clause--how much he had spent on repairs. Connect the two clauses.

> Tom asked Jane how often she worked overtime.

("How often" acts as a single-word adverb)
> N-1 + action verb + N-3 (how often) N-1 + action verb

Process--
> Independent clause--Tom asked Jane (something)
> Clause to be connected--she worked overtime how often

Move the adverb "how often" to the beginning of its clause--how often she worked overtime. Connect the two clauses.

Interrogators

Another two-job connector is the Interrogator. It is used when the verb in the main clause indicates by its meaning that a question is being asked. The interrogator looks exactly like the relative adverbs we have seen above, but these are given interrogative coloring by the preceding verb. This happens only after a few verbs--"ask, wonder, inquire, want to know."

Direct and Indirect Questions

Direct question--
> My husband asked, "Where did you park the car?"
> N-1 + action verb (where) N-1 + action verb + N-3

Notice the comma after the key verb "asked," the capitalization of the first word in the question, the question mark, and the use of quotation marks.

Process--
> Independent clause--My husband asked (something.)
> Clause to be connected--you did park the car where

We follow the same procedure as with relators--the connector is moved to the beginning of its clause--where you did park the car
Since this is a question, we reverse the order of the auxiliary and the subject--where did you park the car
Now we connect the clauses and add the punctuation and capitalization.
The auxiliary "did" is necessary because English no longer allows the simple reversal ("parked you") for a question. (See "Do as an Auxiliary" in Chapter 2.)

Indirect question--
> My husband asked where I parked the car.
> N-1 + action verb (where) N-1 + action verb + N-3

Notice the lack of the capitalization and special punctuation used in the direct question as well as the absence of the auxiliary "did." Moreover, we do not reverse the subject and verb in an indirect question.
The whole interrogative burden is borne by the verb "asked." The same sentence with a non-interrogative verb will be a statement, not an indirect question--
> My husband knew where I parked the car.

The other interrogators work in the same way--they depend upon the question-coloring of the verb to create indirect questions--
> I wondered when I would find a good job
> N-1 + action verb (when) N-1 + action verb + N-3

(direct question--I asked myself, "When will I find a good job?")
> Our guide inquired why the museum was not open.
> N-1 + action verb (why) N-1 + link verb + adj

(direct question--Our guide inquired, "Why is the museum closed?")
> The children want-to-know how the puppet can talk.
> N-1 + action verb (how) N-1 + action verb

(direct question--The children asked, "How can the puppet talk?")
> The children want-to-know how often they can see the same show.
> N-1 + action verb (how often) N-1 + action verb + N-3

(direct question--The children asked, "How often can we see the same show?"
> Their father wants-to-know how much their lunch will cost.
> N-1 + action verb (how much) N-1 + action verb

(direct question--Their father asked, "How much will their lunch cost?")

If these interrogators do not follow a question-asking verb, they are not interrogators at all; they are relative adverbs. In each case, however, they are acting as connectors of a dependent clause to an independent clause in order to create supersentences.

Summary of Connectors

1. To connect sentence patterns of equal importance--
   Use Coordinate Conjunctions "and, but, or, nor" and the semicolon. We can then say that the supersentence consists of two independent clauses.
2. To combine two patterns so that one is more important than the other—

a) Use Subordinate Conjunctions (which only do one job)--
"after, although, as, as if, because, before, if, since, than,
that, though, till, until, unless, whether, while."
We can then say the supersentence consists of one independent
clause and one subordinate clause.

b) Use Relators (which do two jobs) to add descriptive or
identifying detail) ("which, that, who"), possession ("whose"),
or adverbial information about time, place, location, method,
or extent ("where, when, why, how, how much, how often").
We can then say that the supersentence consists of one
independent clause and one relative clause (a kind of dependent
clause).

c) Use Interrogators (which also do a second job) if we wish to
create an indirect question.
We can then say that the supersentence consists of one
independent clause and an indirect question (another kind of
dependent clause).

Exercise 22

Describe the construction of the following supersentences as
combinations of independent clause, subordinate clause, relative
clause or indirect question. Finding the connectors will make this
possible. (The internal punctuation which could offer clues has been
omitted.)

For example—Nobody asked why the bus driver looked
like a man who had seen a ghost.
independent clause—nobody asked (something)
indirect question--why the bus driver looked like a man
who had seen a ghost
relative clause—who had seen a ghost

Connectors are "why" and "who."

1. Because the drought has lasted a long time, the vast swamp has
   been drying out and the alligators which depend upon water have
   been showing signs of stress.
2. All of the tourists whose baggage had been lost lined up at the front
   desk while the hotel manager shouted at someone at the other end
   of the phone connection.
3. The detective who had no sympathy for anyone in the bereaved
   family questioned everyone over and over again although no one
   had anything more to report.
4. The time has come when you will need a driver's license.
5. I wondered why we had to get up so early since our bus would not
   leave until lunch time.

6. The reporters who were covering the races wanted to know whose canoe had turned over in the swift current.
7. We waited in the shade of a large oak tree while the mechanic looked at the engine of our car.
8. The children kept asking their mother where she had put the candy which they had collected on Halloween.
9. In the confusion of their move to a new house, nobody in the family noticed that the puppy had been left behind.
10. The real estate salesman drove Walter around the town all afternoon but Walter did not show any interest in the houses for sale.

Exercise 23

Identify each of the following as a supersentence or a sentence fragment. Turn the fragments into acceptable sentences either by eliminating the connector or by adding or completing an independent clause.

1. Although the students had double-checked their experiments during the chemistry exam.
2. Suddenly when lightning struck the building, the lights went out.
3. A traveling circus which had set up its tent on the outskirts of the village.
4. The most dangerous part of the trail where the elephant had dislodged some rocks.
5. The students talked among themselves while the lecturer picked up his notes which he had dropped on the floor.
6. Because the tour guide was lingering over his beer at the little cafe on the corner, the band of tourists entered the shops that lined the esplanade.
7. The singer who was very particular about the temperature of the auditorium.
8. Many pioneer wagons carrying whole families of settlers headed for the frontier.
9. Broadway's theater critics who were usually skeptical of foreign headliners.
10. Since we all needed a good night's sleep after our strenuous afternoon running in the senior citizens' marathon.

Exercise 24

Make each of the following pairs into supersentences using the connector that the sense suggests. In some cases it may be necessary to drop a repeated noun or to use a pronoun instead of a noun.

It is also possible to interrupt the independent clause by inserting the dependent clause before the independent clause is complete.

> The house-- where Mozart was born-- is a tourist attraction.
>
> The politician-- who lost the election--canceled his hotel reservation.

1. Joe dislikes cold weather. He has recently taken up skiing.
   a) Use a connector showing equality with contrast .
   b) Use a connector that shows inequality and notes a concession.
2. The two sisters traveled to Europe. They stayed for six months.
   a) Use a connector that shows inequality and that acts as a pronoun.
   b) Use a connector that shows equality of the two patterns.
3. These rosebushes will bloom for me. I'll give up gardening.
   Use a connector that shows equality but makes one sentence an alternative to the other.
4. The camper had been unforgivably careless. The camper caused the forest fire.
   a) Making the first sentence the main pattern and making the second the dependent one, use a connector that shows inequality and acts as a pronoun.
   b) Using the same connector, make the second pattern the main one and the first pattern the dependent one.
5. Howard's wife liked to swim. Howard's family moved to the seashore.
   a) Use a connector that creates inequality and shows cause-result.
   b) Use another connector that does the same.
6. Most dogs like to paddle in the lake. Cats will never go into the water.
   a) Use a connector that creates equality and shows contrast.
   b) Use a connector that creates inequality and shows concession.
7. The judge asked a question. "How long have you been driving?" Join the two sentences by making the direct question into an indirect one.
8. You plan to go to college. You should take high school more seriously.
   a) Use a connector creating inequality and suggesting a condition.
   b) Use a connector creating inequality and suggesting cause.
9. The child wanted to know (something.) "When will you read me a story?"

Join the two sentences by making the direct question into an indirect one.

10. We have all learned (something.) We have learned why the glaciers are melting.
    Join the two sentences by using the existing WH word and deleting unnecessary words.

The nature of the connective makes all the difference. Some permit the two statements to be reversed. Some do not. Some force the second statement to interrupt the main statement and others do not. Obviously, connectives are powerful words.
.

Although we have discussing the joining of two sentence patterns in various ways, the fact is that most writing—particularly writing intended for print—is more complicated. Joining three or four patterns with various kinds of connectors to produce an intricate supersentence is common. For example, we can have a subordinate clause, a relative clause, and a buried question all in one supersentence. We can have two or more independent clauses (connected by a coordinate conjunction) plus a subordinate clause and two relative clauses. The possibilities are many, but every supersentence must contain at least one independent clause. Otherwise we have a Sentence Fragment.

The best writing is a mixture of sentence structures. How this mixture is achieved depends upon the writer's feel for sentence rhythms usually developed over the years by native users of English. A newcomer to the language can acquire this skill by continual reading of non-fiction as found in carefully edited newspapers and magazines. Reading aloud to oneself helps to master sentence rhythms.

Reading fiction, while pleasurable, will not necessarily develop the skills needed for everyday writing. Novelists often make free with the language as virtuoso violinists or pianists do with music. Some esteemed American novelists like Henry James and William Faulkner are famous for their intricate sentences which can try the reader's patience. Others, as Ernest Hemingway did, go to the other extreme and use overly simple straightforward sentences which can become tiresome.

For our practical purposes, effective writing consists of sentences that are neither too complicated nor too simple. It is wise to assume that the reader will be someone who is in a hurry but who still wants the respect that careful writing implies.

CHAPTER 5

SPECIAL TOPICS
Multiple-Use Words, Free-lance Words, Negatives Revisited,
Interrogatives Summary, Imperatives, the Passive Voice

Multiple-Use Words

Since language operates in the everyday world of human beings, who
are often unpredictable, it lacks the beautiful precision of mathematics.
Therefore any attempt to sort out and classify units of language--
words--is bound to run into repetitions, exceptions, and even
contradictions. One of the problems is that of multiple-use words that
act one way in one sentence, another way in another sentence, and
even a third and fourth way in other sentences. This is particularly true
in the case of the servant words--prepositions, conjunctions, relators,
interrogators, place-holders, and the infinitive marker. It is helpful to
think of them as twins, triplets, quadruplets, and quintuplets.

Although we have already met some of the key words in this chapter, it
is worth our while to see them again in a different context.

Twins
Words That Do Either of Two Jobs

1. "After" as Preposition or Conjunction--
    The program will begin after-lunch.
(preposition forming prepositional phrase)
    The program will begin after-lunch-has-been-served.
(subordinate conjunction connecting dependent clause to main
clause)

"Before" as Preposition or Conjunction--
    The program will begin before-lunch.
(preposition forming prepositional phrase)
    The program will begin before-lunch-is-served.
(subordinate conjunction connecting dependent clause to main
clause)

2. "There" as Adverb or Place-holder--
> The gardener planted the bush there, not here.

(adverb of place modifying verb "planted")
> There are billions of stars in the sky.

(place-holder--a meaningless word of no grammatical importance put in the place of the subject of the sentence so that the subject can be put after the verb for greater emphasis) This is useful in a long sentence where we might forget the subject as we work our way through the words that follow.

In a sentence where "there" holds the subject position, the verb is usually some form of "be" (meaning "exist"). Although normal word order can be used--"Billions of stars are in the sky"--most of us would use the "there" place-holder because it softens the pedantic tone of the sentence.

Sometimes, with "be" as the verb, the place-holder is required because the normal word order will not result in a usable sentence.
> There is no rest for the weary.

> No rest for the weary is.

(unusable sentence because a link verb requires a complement-- Nn-1 pred adj, or pred adv.)

Exercise 25

In each of the following sentences, eliminate the place-holder "there" by putting the true subject in front of the verb. Does this make the sentence more or less acceptable?

1. There is no excuse for reckless driving.
2. There are several scholarship winners among these high school
     graduates.
3. There comes a time when you must pay your credit card bill.
4. There will be music and dancing at our annual gala.
5. There seems to be only one solution for your problem.

3. "To" as Preposition or Infinitive Marker
> Wilson talked to-the-stranger.

(preposition forming prepositional phrase)
> Wilson wanted to-leave-early.

(infinitive marker)

When "to" is set in front of any verb, it automatically creates an infinitive that can never act as the sentence verb. For example," Fish swim" is a sentence with a full verb. "Fish to swim" is no longer a sentence because the "to" has demoted the verb to a lower status. An infinitive can act only as a noun, an adjective, or an adverb.

Caution--The word "to" should not be confused with "too" or "two." Although they all sound alike, they have no grammatical connection.

"Too" is an adverb that modifies an adjective or another adverb, as in "too hot" or "too slowly." "Two" always represents the number 2.

Exercise 26

Locate every "to" and decide how it is being used.
1. When no one answered the doorbell, our dog began to bark.
2. The new waiter was too eager to clear away our plates.
3. The traffic officer gave tickets to the two drivers who had driven through the red light.
4. Soon our family will be going to our country house to start a long vacation.
5. To understand the problem, you need to listen to the professor's explanation.

Triplets
Words That Can Do Any One of Three Jobs

1. WH-Club members as Connectors, Indirect Questioners, and Parts of Speech (pronoun, adjective, adverb) (See upcoming "versatility of WH-Club members.")

2. "It" as Personal Pronoun, Empty-word Subject, and Place-holder
    I had a glass vase but Elsie broke it.
(called a "personal" pronoun although it never refers to a person)
    It is raining.
    It is ten o'clock.
(idiomatic use when referring to weather or time. "It" has no meaning.)
    It is true that honesty is the best policy.
    It is hard to accept a shortage of gasoline.
"It" (like "there" above) as a place-holder is generally used when the subject of the sentence is a subordinate clause beginning with "that" or when the subject is an infinitive or an infinitive phrase. Putting a complex grammatical structure like a clause or a phrase at the end of the sentence makes it easier for the reader or listener to connect it with the key word in the sentence--the predicate adjective. This postponement of the subject is so common that the normal word order (clause or phrase in the subject position) sounds awkward--"That honesty is the best policy is true." "To accept a shortage of gasoline is hard." We would seldom use these versions.

Exercise 27

Explain the use of every "it" in the following sentences.
1. Ask not for whom the bell tolls. It tolls for you.
2. I couldn't ride my bike because it had a flat tire.

3. It is important to pay attention in a math class.
4. It was eight o'clock before I noticed that it was snowing outside.
5. Eddie's pet snake escaped and it was almost midnight before he found it.

3. "Up" as Preposition or Adverb or Particle
> A stray dog ran up-the-stairs.

(preposition forming prepositional phrase)
> Stand up when your name is called.

(adverb modifying the verb "stand")
> I hope you will keep up the good work.

(a particle changing the meaning of the verb from "keep" to "continue")
> The clerk will wrap up your package.

(a particle intensifying the meaning of the verb)

Exercise 28

Explain the use of "up" in the following sentences.
1. I hope someone will clean up this mess.
2. At last the parade came up the avenue.
3. You should buckle up your seat belt before you drive.
4. Take the elevator up but walk down.
5. I had to give up my gym membership.

Quadruplets
A Word That Does Any One of Four Jobs

"That" as Demonstrative Adjective, Demonstrative Pronoun, Relator, or Subordinate Conjunction
> I like that bracelet better than this bracelet.
> I like that better than this.

("That"as a demonstrative adjective or demonstrative pronoun points out something farther away in a comparison. It is often used with "this" which indicates the nearer thing.)
Sometimes it is an adjective modifying a noun--"that bracelet"-- and sometimes it is a pronoun standing alone.
> I like those bracelets better than these bracelets.
> I like those better than these.

(The plural form of the demonstrative "that" is "those." The plural form of the demonstrative "this" is "these.")
> That may be easy for you, but not for me.

(pronoun referring to something previously mentioned)
> Paris is a city that I know well.

Here "that" is a relator connecting a dependent clause to a main clause while doing a grammatical job (N-3) in its own clause--
> Paris is a city + I know that well.

Reminder--No matter what grammatical job a relator is doing, it always appears at the beginning of its dependent clause because of its importance as a connector.

I hope that you will accept my invitation.

("That" is a subordinate conjunction. It connects the dependent clause--"you will accept my invitation"--with the main clause--"I hope"(something). It is not a relator in this sentence because it is not doing a second job. It can, in fact, be omitted, although it is always understood. "I hope you will accept my invitation.")

Exercise 29

Label each "that" in the following sentences as a demonstrative, a pronoun, a relator, or a subordinate conjunction.
1. I wish I could drive that car.
2. This lamp is less expensive than that.
3..The landlord told us that we would have to vacate the apartment.
4. Your first summer at camp--please tell me about that.
5. The river that flooded the town had been rising for three days.

Quintuplets
A Word That Does Any One of Five Jobs

"Do" as main verb, helping verb, replacement verb, negation helper, and question helper

My daughter did her homework.

("do" as main verb)

I do (so) like dogs.

(adds emphasis to the main verb--with or without "so")

You ought to work as hard as I (do)

You ought to work as hard as I work.

You ought to work as hard as I.

(This "do" often omitted because it is understood. It is used to avoid repetition of main verb in a comparison.

The king does not listen to his advisers.

(used in order to allow addition of "not")

Do the younger children need help?

(used in order to ask a question)

Exercise 30

State the use of a form of "do" in each of the following sentences.
1. Do you like classical music?
2. Some of the children did not listen to the new teacher.
3. The handyman does necessary repairs for us.
4. The younger students in our class worked harder than we did.

5. Some birds do not go south for the winter.
6. I really do expect to find a job soon.
7. In this emergency everyone should do his job carefully.
8. The inspectors did not give the new building their approval.
9. Did Mr. Foster win the election?
10. When does the parade start?

VERSATILITY OF WH- CLUB MEMBERS

(WH-Club members--who/whom/ whose, which, what, where, when, why, how)

The range of jobs performed by WH- Club members merits a revisit.

1. In simple (one-pattern) sentences, they do 2 jobs at the same time--interrogators and particular parts of speech (pronoun, adjective, adverb) in direct questions--

> Who are you? (pronoun as N-1)
> Whose cell phone is ringing? (adjective modifying "phone")
> Whom are you looking for? (pronoun as object of preposition "for"--You are looking for whom?)
> Which sport do you prefer? (adjective modifying "sport")
> What do you want? (pronoun as N-3--You want what?)
> Where are you going? (adverb modifying "going")
> When does the show start? (adverb modifying "start")
> Why has the train stopped? (adverb modifying "stopped")
> How can I help you? (adverb modifying "help")

2. In supersentences these words are called relators because they take on the additional job of relating (connecting) one clause to another. This adds up to 3 jobs at the same time. They do all their work in the second clause--connecting, (first job), acting as a part of speech in their own clause (second job) and either asking a question or giving information (third job).

Third job--
a) asking a question. This occurs only when the main verb (in the first clause) sets up a question-asking situation. The most common of these main verbs are "asked, inquired, wondered, wanted to know, do know, do not know, forgot, explained." The result is an indirect question. The punctuation for this kind of supersentence is always a period. In the following examples, notice that the verb in the indirect question sometimes shifts into the past tense because a previous event is being reported.

I don't know who you are.
(pronoun as N-1-- you are who-- direct question--Who are you?)
Jerry asked whose cell phone was ringing.
(adjective modifying "phone"--direct question--Whose cell phone is ringing?)
I'm looking for someone whom I can trust
pronoun as N-3--I can trust whom--direct question--Whom can I trust?)
Maria didn't know which bus she should take.
(adjective modifying "bus"--she should take which bus-- direct question--Which bus should I take?)
Jim asked what caused the accident.
(pronoun as N-1) direct question--What caused the accident?)
Mama forgot where she put her keys.
(adverb modifying verb "put"--she put keys where)--direct question--Where did I put my keys?)
No one knew when dinner would be served.
(adverb modifying verb "served"--direct question--When will dinner be served?)
The man asked why a seat was not available.
(adverb modifying verb "was"-- direct question--Why is a seat not available? or Why isn't a seat available?)
My father wondered how he could improve his golf stroke.
(adverb modifying verb "improve" --direct question--How can I improve my golf stroke?)
b) giving information—
This is the creek where we often swam.
"where we often swam" is a clause acting as an adjective by modifying "creek." (At the same time, within its own clause, "where" is an adverb modifying "swam.")
I'm going to the movies when I finish my homework.
" when I finish my homework" is a clause acting as an adverb by modifying the verb "going." Within its own clause it is also acting as an adverb by modifying the verb "finish.")
The neighbors knew how Mr. Brown had made his fortune.
"how Mr. Brown had made his fortune" is a clause acting as N-3 for the verb "knew." Within its own clause, "how" is an adverb modifying the verb "made."

Exercise 31

Identify each WH- (and How) word as interrogator or relator. The end punctuation for each sentence has been omitted.
1. Who is the man with the beard
2. I don't care who you are

3. The person who left the message is an old friend
4. Which car is yours
5. We wondered which restaurant would be open
6. Who is going to repair the broken window
7. I didn't know where to put the crates
8. No one asked where the magistrate had gone
9. Joe found out why Dad had hidden the car keys
10. The coach told the freshman how he could qualify for the team

Free-lance words

A few words with no grammatical significance frequently turn up in sentences to affect meanings or to respond to particular situations--

Politeness signal--please, sorry
> Please sit down. Sit down, please.
> Sorry, I didn't mean to push you.

Response to a question--yes, no, maybe
> Are you going to the party? Yes. (No. Maybe)

Hesitator--well
> Well, I think it's time for me to leave.

Interjection--Wow! Gosh! (many others)
> Gee whiz! That was a narrow escape.

Negatives revisited

In addition to adding "not" or "n't," there are several other ways of expressing negation.

1. adverbs of negation and near-negation--"never, seldom, rarely, scarcely ever, barely, hardly ever"

Notice that these adverbs are placed between the subject word and the verb.
> I never carry an umbrella.
> I seldom carry an umbrella.
> I rarely carry an umbrella.
> I scarcely ever carry an umbrella.
> I barely caught my commuter train.

2. negative determiner (precedes the noun)--"no"
> No club members paid their dues on time.
> My brother has no money.

3. negative pronoun-- "no one, nobody, none"
> No one answered the doorbell.
> The judge said nobody was guilty.
> None of these candidates will be elected.

4. negative prefix on a noun--"in-, im-, ir-, non-, un-"

You are ineligible for the position.
That custom is immoral.
Your procedure is highly irregular
That purchase is non-returnable.
The mayor was unwilling to make a speech.
5. negative coordinators--"neither...nor..., not...neither..."
Neither the king nor his council listened to my suggestion.
The king did not listen to my suggestion and neither did his council.

Exercise 32

Make each of the following sentences negative in as many ways as possible.
1. The basketball team will play many games this season.
2. The squad members were ready to help put out the fire.
3. Our neighbors always park their car in their driveway.
4. Every passenger on the train was reading a newspaper.
5. I know exactly what your score is.
6. With enough preparation you will be able to go to college.
7. Aunt Rosa might like maple syrup on her vanilla ice cream.
8. Either a goat or an elephant ruined our front lawn.
9. Many people enjoy a cocktail before dinner.
10. This hotel will allow pets in your room.

Interrogatives summary

There are several kinds of interrogative sentences in English.
1. The yes/no question
2. The information-seeking question
3. The tag question--a statement followed by an interrogative tag. It seeks approval, not information.
4. The indirect question
5. The rhetorical question
6. The false question

1. The yes/no question--
This expects a yes or no answer, although the answer may turn out to be "maybe, sometimes, seldom, never..."
a) When the verb has a helper, the helper is moved to the beginning of the sentence--Has the guest of honor arrived?
Can we go home now?
Will the train stop at my station?
Should the fish be packed in ice?
b) When the verb has no helper, we add a form of "do"--
Do you have any money?

Did your nephew pass his exams?

Does that old car stall often?

c) When the verb is "be," the subject and verb are simply reversed--

Are you hungry?

Was the campaign a success?

Is this your favorite color?

When the main verb is "be" and it has a helper, it is the helper that reverses with the subject--

Is the teacher being unfair?

Has the salesman been helpful?

2. The information-seeking question--

This begins with one of the WH- words (or How) .

Who are you?

Where is my driving license?

When the verb has a helper, we begin with a WH- word and reverse the subject and the helper.

What is he doing?

How can we help you?

Why is the child crying?

3. Tag question --

This looks like an interrogative since it ends with a question mark. However, it is not really a question. It is not asking for information. It is a device for making a statement without sounding too assertive. It occurs most often in spoken English, but occasionally turns up in informal writing.

A tag question can be affirmative or negative. If the original statement is affirmative, the tag is negative. If the original statement is negative, the tag is affirmative. The verb forms in the tag are auxiliaries, helpers, or modals.

That program was boring, wasn't it?

All children like pizza, don't they?

Your aunt will be glad to see us, won't she?

I've made that mistake before, haven't I?

That program wasn't boring, was it?

All children don't like pizza, do they?

Your aunt won't be glad to see us, will she?

I haven't made that mistake before, have I?

4. Indirect question--

A question can sometimes be buried in a statement. This occurs when, instead of asking a question ourselves, we simply report that someone else did so. The absence of a question mark indicates that this is not an actual interrogative and no answer is expected.

Who will go?—direct question (answer expected)

The leader asked who would go—indirect question (no answer expected)

Note that the modal has shifted into the past tense because the sentence is reporting a past event.

> Who broke the dish? Mother wanted to know who broke the dish.
>
> What is wrong? The nurse asked what was wrong.
>
> How can anyone answer that question? I wondered how anyone could answer that question.

Note that when there is a modal plus a main verb, it is the modal that shifts into the past tense.

> What do the people want? The chairman asked what the people wanted.
>
> Who designed that dress? I asked who designed that dress.
>
> How does she stay so young? Everyone wondered how she stayed so young.

5. Rhetorical question—

A rhetorical question is one that does not want an answer. Whether spoken or written, it is used purely for effect—sometimes to announce indirectly what the speaker or writer is going to discuss.

> What is the result of our national neglect of highway maintenance? (The speaker--or writer-- is going to tell us in the next sentence.)

Sometimes a rhetorical question is used to revive the attention of the reader or listener, particularly when the speech or essay is long and involved. In this case, an abrupt question can be effective.

It is considered extremely rude for a member of the audience to call out an answer to a speaker's rhetorical question.

6. False question—

In spoken English, a demand or wish can be put into question form for the sake of politeness.

> Would you mind if I sit here? (I'd like to sit here.)
>
> Can you lend me a hand with this? (Please help me.)
>
> Do you have an extra program? (I need a program.)
>
> Is anyone using this chair? (I want this chair.)
>
> Would you mind if I asked you to move over? (Please move over.)

Exercise 33

Turn each of the following into a yes/no question.
1. The basketball game had ended in a tie.
2. Her husband can take time off from work.
3. The charter fishing boat crashed into the dock.
4. Raw meat should be kept in the refrigerator.
5. The elephants are waiting for their food.
6. The price of a first-night ticket is too high.

7. The decision of the committee had proved to be a mistake.
8. Without our help, Ed's search for a job might have ended in failure.
9. The builder filed plans for a community hospital.
10. Tom was conspicuous in a red plaid jacket.

Exercise 34

See if you can write six information-seeking questions using the following facts—
Because his own car broke down, the thief made his getaway at high noon in a car which his confederate had parked around the corner from the bank

Exercise 35

Turn each of the following into a tag question.
1. Alaska is part of the continental United States.
2. Swimming with dolphins can be a thrilling experience.
3. The study of history will be enlightening.
4. Her gymnastic performance was not very impressive.
5. Those tennis players are not members of our country club.

Exercise 36

Write a direct question based on each of the following indirect questions.
1. We asked the usher how long the intermission would be.
2. The examiner wanted to know where my application had been filed.
3. The senior officials inquired why the supplies had run out.
4. All of us wondered when the next train was due.
5. I forgot to ask the secretary who her boss was.

Exercise 37

What is the underlying request or demand in each of the following false questions?
1. May I share this table?
2. Do you need all those chairs?
3. Would you mind if I ask you to move over?
4. Have you finished with this newspaper?
5. Can you spare one of those napkins?

Imperatives

An imperative sentence may be as gentle as a suggestion or as sharp as a military order. It can even masquerade as a simple statement of fact that is meant as a hint. The form used depends upon the situation or the relationship between the speaker/writer and the listener/reader.

> I think it would be a good idea for you to phone your mother. (suggestion)
> Watch tour step. (command)
> I'm just too tired to clean up the kitchen. (disguised request)

Imperatives in written English occur most often on signs ("Watch your step") and in the printed directions that come with machines and appliances ("Turn off the power when the machine is not in use.") Occasionally an imperative can turn up in an editorial, a political rant, or a magazine article. It may or may not be disguised as a suggestion.

> Who designs those dresses?
> I asked who designed those dresses.
> Wake up, America!
> Let's have some action on that tax bill.
> Follow the money trail to the State House.

For some possibilities in phrasing a request or demand, see the "walk the dog" sentences in Overview.

The Passive Voice

The Passive Voice is a common misuse of a sentence pattern that contains a transitive verb. The normal transitive-verb sentence is said to be in the Active Voice—it is full of action.

> The man bought a ticket. N-1 + Vtr + N-3
> The man gave his wife the ticket. N-1 + Vtr + N-2 + N-3
> John's will named his wife the beneficiary. N-1 + Vtr + N-3 + Nn-3

In these three sentence patterns, the subject (N-1) is the doer of the action. The verb transfers the action from the subject to the direct object (N-3). Additional information may be supplied by the N-2 or the Nn-3. This transfer of action produces a dynamic forward-moving effect that keeps the reading process moving in the right direction.

Consider the following versions of these sentences—
> A ticket was bought by the man.
> The ticket was given to his wife by the man.
> His wife was named the beneficiary by John's will.

His wife was named the beneficiary.

Three undesirable things have happened. First, two extra words have been added—"by" and a form of the auxiliary "be." They add nothing to the meaning and serve merely to slow the sentence down.

Second, the receiver of the action has been moved to the subject position and the doer of the action has been demoted to being the object of a preposition in a phrase at the end of the sentence. Notice that in the #4 version, the prepositional phrase containing the original subject has been dropped from the sentence.

Third, the main verb is now in its past participle form.

The bounce is gone. The forward movement of the sentence has been turned into a backward movement because we have to look for the subject at the end of the sentence and then match it with the verb and object. If the subject has been dropped, we have lost some information.

This backward movement is called the Passive Voice. It produces clumsy sentences and is to be avoided. It is, however, a way of writing that is easy to fall into and one that can become a habit.

It is important to recognize the passive when it occurs in your writing and to know how to change it to the active voice.

Recognition---The main verb will always be preceded by a form of "be" acting as a helper. The main verb will be the past participle form. The receiver (rather than the doer) of the action will be in the subject position.

The doer of the action will be the object of the preposition "by," with the resulting phrase placed on the right-hand side of the verb. Alternately, the doer of the action—now in a prepositional phrase-- will have been deleted.

Passive--

> The cost of the snow removal was estimated by the mayor.

Change to active voice--

Step 1--Delete the form of "be" that is acting as the helping verb.

> The cost of the snow removal estimated by the mayor

Step 2--Delete "by" and move "the mayor" to its normal subject position.

> The mayor the cost of the snow removal estimated.

Step 3--Move the verb to its normal position immediately after the subject

> The mayor estimated the cost of the snow removal.

Step 4--Change the verb from its past participle form to its simple past. This will only be necessary in the case of irregular verbs, since the past tense form and the past participle form of regular verbs are identical.

Irregular verb--

    The race was run by four strangers.
    Four strangers ran the race.

The GET Passive--

There is another way of forming the passive which may be heard in informal speech, although it is generally frowned upon. In the "get" passive, the verb "get" is used as the auxiliary instead of "be."

    The train got derailed by a defective signal. (The train was derailed by a defective signal.)
    Our tax money'll get spent by those politicians. (Our tax money will be spent by those politicians.)

Check your own writing from time to time to see if you have begun using the verb "be" as a helper in front of a past participle. This is the indicator of a passive sentence. Wherever you find this, follow the steps listed above to turn passive sentences into active ones. Reminder—A sentence that does not contain an N-3 (direct object) does not fall into active-passive territory. Therefore, sentences that are based on the following patterns cannot be made passive--
N-1+ Vintr, N-1+Vlink + Nn-1, N-1 + Vlink + Pred Adj or Adv.

Exercise 38

Decide which of the following sentences are active, which are passive, and which fall outside the territory.
1. Three blasts of the siren gave the village a warning.
2. Two young women were sitting on the veranda of the old house.
3. A growling dog watched the stranger's approach.
4. America was first settled by the Spanish.
5. Thanksgiving is celebrated as a family holiday.
6. The man's face turned red with anger.
7. Election Day is not considered a holiday.
8. I inherited this locket from my grandmother.
 9. Elliott was named treasurer by the board of directors.
10. This medal was presented to me by the governor.
11. The cause of the accident was determined almost at once.
12. First aid was administered to the accident victim immediately.

Exercise 39

Change the passive sentences into active ones, adding or deleting words as necessary.

CHAPTER 6

EMBEDDING

In our exploration of English sentences we began with the essential two, three or four words that form the sentence pattern.

Fish swim.
Heat melts ice.
Mama gave Eddie (a) cookie.
Voters elected Lincoln president.
Australia is (a) continent.
Oceans are salty.
(The) taxi is here/ (The) time (to act) is now.

We then saw how details can be added, not only by single words, but also by small packages (phrases) or large packages (clauses).

(Some) fish swim (rapidly).
Heat (from-the-sun) melts ice (on-the-sidewalk).
(Putting-down-her-wooden-spoon), Mama gave Eddie (a) cookie.
Mama gave Eddie (a) cookie (to-keep-him-quiet).
Voters (who-had-registered) elected Lincoln president.
Australia is a continent (that-is-also-an-island).

We are now ready to see how packages can fit into other packages. This is known as embedding. Any kind of word package can fit inside another package no matter how big or small. (We have already seen examples of embedded prepositional phrases in Chapter 3.)
A clause can contain an embedded phrase--

where the treasure had been buried (under-a-rock)

A phrase can contain an embedded clause--

under-the-rock (where-the-treasure-had-been-buried)

Any number of embedded packages can be found in a single sentence—

The policeman (blowing-his-whistle) ordered me (to-turn-right) (at-the-next-corner) (which-was-deserted).

Any number of packages can be embedded within one another, as the previous sentence illustrates—

The policeman blowing his whistle--noun cluster--head word "policeman"

blowing his whistle--verbal adjective phrase

his whistle--noun cluster--head word "whistle"

to turn right at the next corner which was deserted infinitive phrase

at the next corner which was deserted--prepositional phrase

the next corner which was deserted--noun cluster--head word "corner"

which was deserted--adjective clause modifying "corner"

was deserted—verb cluster—head word "deserted"

Even a sentence as simple as "His car hit the tree in my yard" can contain embedded packages--

"His car"--noun cluster (package) + "hit" (single word verb) + "the tree in my yard"--noun cluster (package) with an embedded prepositional phrase "in my yard" which in turn has an embedded noun cluster "my yard."

Word Packages in an Imaginary Hierarchy

The presence of a verb form in a word packages automatically makes it more important grammatically than a package without a verb form.

Basic question for a word group (a word package)-- Is it independent? (Can it stand alone?) If it were dropped from the sentence, would the sentence pattern be damaged? Does it contain a full-fledged verb that has a visible subject? If the answer to these questions is Yes, we have a sentence pattern, which is an independent clause. All other word groups are of lesser value grammatically.

If we assigned a monetary value to each package, how would it rate?

1. sentence pattern---an independent clause= 1 dollar (can stand alone)
2. subordinate (dependent) clause =90 cents (a full sentence pattern made subordinate)
3. relative clause or indirect question= 90 cents (a full sentence pattern made subordinate)
4. verb cluster = 80 cents (could be the predicate in an independent sentence or in a subordinate sentence pattern or merely part of a modifying verbal phrase)
5. noun cluster = 80 cents (could be subject or complement in an independent sentence or a subordinate sentence pattern or merely the object of a preposition)
6. pair or series = 80 cents (could be any part of a sentence)— sometimes droppable and sometimes not droppable

7. infinitive phrase =80 cents (could be the subject or the complement in a sentence or merely a modifier)—sometimes droppable and sometimes not droppable
8. verbal noun phrase = 80 cents (usually the subject or complement in a sentence, although on occasion merely the object of a preposition)
9. verbal adjective phrase= 25 cents (never more than an adjectival modifier—droppable-- but has some importance because it contains a verb form)
10. adjective cluster =15 cents (usually a noun modifier—droppable-- but occasionally the predicate adjective after a linking verb—not droppable then)
11. adverb cluster = 10 cents (modifier--droppable)
12. prepositional phrase = 10 cents (modifier—droppable)

This scale will be valid only if each package does not contain another package. The reality of everyday language is such that any kind of package can contain any other kind of package. Also, the degree of embedding can be as extreme as the writer wishes. It is inadvisable, however, to overdo the embedding and jam too many packages into each other. The result can be an overloaded sentence.

Embedding

In the following examples, the numbers refer to the numbers of the packages listed in the hierarchy above..

A.   on the street (where the accident occurred)
This is a #12 containing #3 --a prepositional phrase with an embedded relative clause.
Each of these two constructions contains further embedding--
the prepositional phrase contains a noun cluster—
          the street where the accident occurred
The relative clause contains an independent clause—
          the accident occurred
the independent clause contains a noun cluster—
          the street.

on the street where the accident occurred
     the street where the accident occurred
          where the accident occurred
                the accident occurred
                the accident

B.   telling the boy that the big dog was friendly

This is either a #8 or #9 (we cannot tell a verbal noun phrase from a verbal adjective phrase without its use in a sentence). Whichever kind of verbal phrase it is, it contains an embedded noun cluster--

      the boy
and a subordinate clause--
      that the big dog was friendly
The subordinate clause contains an independent clause--
      the big dog was friendly
This independent clause contains a noun cluster--
      the big dog
and a verb cluster--
      was friendly

    telling the boy that the big dog was friendly
      the boy
          that the big dog was friendly
          the big dog was friendly
          the big dog
            was friendly

C.   to have eaten the last cookie
This is a #7 containing a #4--an infinitive phrase containing a verb cluster—
      have eaten the last cookie
The verb cluster contains a noun cluster—
      the last cookie

to have eaten the last cookie
   have eaten the last cookie
      the last cookie

D.   expensive as a yacht or a plane
This is a #10 containing a #6--an adjective cluster with an embedded pair--
The embedded pair--
      a yacht or a plane
contains two noun clusters--
      a yacht
      a plane

expensive as a yacht or a plane
      a yacht or a plane
      a yacht   a plane

E.   a gold medal in its box of blue velvet

This is a #5 containing a #12--a noun cluster containing a prepositional phrase.

. The prepositional phrase contains a noun cluster--
its box of blue velvet
and that noun cluster contains a prepositional phrase--
of blue velvet
and that phrase contains a noun cluster--
blue velvet

a gold medal in its box of blue velvet
in its box of blue velvet
its box of blue velvet
of blue velvet
blue velvet

Even in a relatively simple sentence, all sorts of packaging can occur.

Hoping to save time, Henry ran between the cars speeding on the highway.

Listing all the packages--
a. (Hoping to save time)—verbal adjective phrase modifying "Henry"
b. (to save time)—infinitive phrase acting as noun object of "hoping"
c. (between the cars speeding on the highway)-- prepositional phrase as adverb modifying "ran"
d. (the cars speeding on the highway)--noun cluster with head word "cars"
e. (speeding on the highway)--verbal adjective phrase modifying "cars"
f. (on the highway)--prepositional phrase as adverb modifying "speeding"
g.(the highway)—noun cluster with "highway" as head word

1.   Hoping to save time
to save time
save time
(The adjective phrase contains the infinitive phrase which contains the verb cluster.)

2.   between the cars speeding on the highway
                     the cars speeding on the highway
                          speeding on the highway
                               on the highway
                                    the highway
(The prepositional phrase contains the noun cluster which contains
the verbal adjective phrase which contains a smaller prepositional
phrase which contains the smaller noun cluster.)

There is no relationship between 1. and 2. Each is acting as a separate
modifier in the sentence--1. modifies "Henry." 2..modifies "ran." One
can be dropped from the sentence without affecting the other.
If we drop 1, we have "Henry ran between the cars speeding on the
highway."
If we drop 2, we have "Hoping to save time, Henry ran."
The basic undroppable sentence pattern is "Henry ran." N-1+ Vintr

A more complicated sentence--
          The man standing near the Christmas tree in the
          window of the department store was trying to decorate
          the top branches.

Listing all the packages--
          a. (the man standing near the Christmas tree in the
          window of the department store)--a noun cluster (head
          word "man"), subject of the sentence
          b. (standing near the Christmas tree in the window of the
          department store)--verbal adjective phrase acting as a
          large adjective modifying "man"
          c. (near the Christmas tree in the window of the
          department store)--a prepositional phrase as adverb
          modifying "standing"
          d. (the Christmas tree in the window of the department
          store)--noun cluster with "tree" as head word (object of
          the preposition "near")
          e. (in the window of the department store)--prepositional
          phrase as adjective modifying "tree"
          f. (the window of the department store)--noun cluster with
          "window" as head word (object of preposition "in")
          g. (of the department store)--prepositional phrase as
          adjective modifying "window"
          h. (the department store)--noun cluster with "store" as
          head word (object of preposition "of")
          i. (was trying to decorate the top branches)--verb cluster
          with "trying" as the head word. This cluster is the entire
          predicate of the sentence.

j. (to decorate the top branches)--infinitive phrase acting as the noun object of "trying"

k. (the top branches)--noun cluster with "branches" as head word. The cluster is acting as object of the verb "decorate"

How these packages are embedded--
The subject of the sentence--

a. the man standing near the Christmas tree in the window of the department store

near the Christmas tree in the window of the department store

the Christmas tree in the window of the department store

in the window of the department store

the window of the department store

of the department store
the department store

(This extreme example of complication is not usual in ordinary writing because it can lead to sentences with so much detail that the reader becomes confused.)

The predicate of the sentence--

was trying to decorate the top branches
to decorate the top branches
the top branches

Basic sentence—man tried (to decorate the top branches). N-1 + Vtr + N-3 (the entire infinitive phrase is the N-3.)

Familiarity with word packages makes it easier to vary sentences—
1. (Riding a bicycle) requires skill.—verbal noun phrase
2. (To ride a bicycle) requires skill.—infinitive phrase
3. The boy (on the bicycle) is skillful. –prepositional phrase
4. The boy (riding the bicycle) is skillful.—verbal adjective phrase
5. The boy (who is riding the bicycle) is skillful.—dependent clause

Exercise 40

Identify each of the following items as a whole. Do not dig out buried structures. Use the following labels—dependent clause (can be a subordinate clause, a relative clause or an indirect question—these are all weakened sentence patterns), infinitive phrase, verbal adjective phrase, verbal noun phrase, prepositional phrase, pair or series, noun cluster, verb cluster, adjective cluster, adverb cluster.

1. its first performance in December
2. behind the old freight depot
3. sure about instant approval
4. to be willing to invest in new business
5. which provide care and compassion for needy adults
6. not very often
7. I made the salad and Joan made the cake
8. sponsored by one of the suburban banks
9. since no one was able to make a deposit
10. should have been ready to leave with the rest of us
11. by spending part of the weekend at the movies
12. if they release the album too soon
13. questioning people
14. so rich that he doesn't know the extent of his fortune
15. whom we had invited for dinner
16. can expect it to be crowded every Friday, Saturday, and Sunday
17. through an almost impenetrable jungle
18. swamps full of crocodiles and mosquitoes
19. climbing on the sideboard, standing on the table, or jumping on the couch
20. all too frequently

Exercise 41

Extract and label all packages, if any, embedded in the Exercise 40 constructions.

CHAPTER 7

DISSECTING and REPAIRING SENTENCES

A string of words of words on the page is not necessarily a grammatically acceptable sentence.

Fragment

unacceptable--(The old) fisherman (watching and waiting throughout a long summer)

N-l + --

This is the error known as a sentence fragment.

acceptable-- (The old) fisherman (watching and waiting throughout a long summer) (finally) saw (his son's) ship (on the horizon).

fisherman saw ship-- N- 1 + Vtr + N-3

By adding the two missing elements (the verb and the direct object), we produced a grammatically acceptable sentence.

Fragment

unacceptable--(Because) Wilson was a swimmer

connector +N-l + link verb + Nn-1

Here we have a good sentence pattern but we also have a word (because) that weakens the statement so that it becomes a sentence fragment.

As we saw in Chapter 4, there are three kinds of connectors that can undercut the independence of a sentence pattern--subordinate conjunctions, relators, and interrogators. "Because" is a subordinate conjunction with the job of connecting this statement to an independent sentence pattern which is missing.

acceptable--Because Wilson was a swimmer, he became a lifeguard.

(subord conj) N-l + link verb + Nn-l

+ N-1 + link verb + Nn-1

By adding an independent sentence pattern, we produced an acceptable sentence.

Note--the subordinate conjunction always keeps its place at the start of the subordinate clause even when its clause begins the sentence.

Run-on

> unacceptable--(Our) car skidded (on the icy road) we
> stopped talking
> N-I + Vintr   N-I + Vtr + N-3

Here we have two independent sentence patterns but no connector to join them. This an error known as a run-on sentence.

> acceptable-- When our car skidded on the icy road, we
> stopped talking.

Adding the relative adverb "when" as a connector produces a good sentence.

> (When) + N-1 + Vintr, N-1 + Vtr + N-3

Note--the relative adverb keeps its place at the start of its clause even though it turns out to be the connector.

Dissecting Sentences

Knowing how to uncover the sentence pattern is the first step in learning how to repair unacceptable sentences.
For short simple sentences the process is quick. For wordy sentences and supersentences, the process can take more time.

Short and Simple

First Step— Find the verb, which will be either action or linking. If there are two or three verb forms side by side, it will be the last one that is the main one. Drop the first one or two because they are acting just as helpers. If the main verb that is left ends in "ing," reduce it to its basic form by dropping the "ing."

1. The oceans on our planet are all salty. (The verb is "are.")
2. The people have been voicing their objections. (The verb is "voice.")
3. The hotel might give us a special rate. (The verb is "give.").
4. Johnson will become the next candidate. (The verb is "become.")
5. The new symphony orchestra played expertly for two hours. (The verb is "played.")
6. The taxi will be here soon. (The verb is "be.")
7. The scientist labeled his latest test a success. (The verb is "labeled.")

Second Step--Look to the left of the verb for the subject noun or pronoun. (What is the sentence about?)
1. oceans (We now have "oceans are.")
2. people (We now have "people voice.")
3. hotel (We now have "hotel give.")
4. Johnson (We now have "Johnson become.")

5. orchestra (We now have "orchestra played.")
6. taxi (We now have "taxi be.")
7. scientist (We now have "scientist labeled.")

Third Step— To the right of the verb, in sentences 1-4 and 6-7, we find the word or words we need to complete the message. This completion unit is usually one or two nouns or the combination of pronoun and noun unless there is a linking verb followed by a predicate adjective or an adverb of place or time.

1. salty (We now have "oceans are salty.") N-1 + link verb + predicate adjective
2. objections (We now have "people voice objections.") N-1+ Vtr + N-3
3. us/rate (We now have "hotel give us rate.") N-1 + Vtr + N-2 + N-3
4. candidate (We now have "Johnson become candidate.") N-1 + link verb + Nn-1
5. This sentence ends with two adverbial expressions which should be dropped. ("Expertly" tells How) and ("for-two-hours" tells How long). Descriptive adverbs are never essential. Only an adverb of place or time following a linking verb can be part of a sentence pattern.
6. here (We now have "taxi be here ") N-1 + link verb + adverb/place
7. test/success (We now have "scientist labeled test success) N-1 + Vtr +N-3 + Nn-3

A Longer Process

Reminder--We are looking for grammatical basics. We are not concerned with precise meaning.

Rule 1--Shrink the verb

We start with the verb. When there is a multi-word verb phrase (a main verb with helpers), we reduce it to the present or past tense form. This will be just one word. The helpers will disappear. (See discussion of verb servants in Chapter 2).

"You should have walked more quickly" becomes "You walked more quickly." Then we apply rule 3 below to get "You walked" N-1 + Vintr
"An inexperienced driver/might have caused the accident" becomes "An inexperienced driver caused the accident."
Then we apply rule 2 below to get "driver caused accident" N-1+ Vtr + N -3
"He must have been saving his money for-college" becomes "He saved his money for college." Then we apply rule 3 below to get" He saved money" N-1 + Vtr + N-3

Rule 2--Strip the noun of its servants

Look at all the nouns. Discard any words preceding each one. These servant words (See Chapter 2) will be giving details about the noun, such as quantity, ownership, size, color, condition, etc.
"Three men departed' becomes "men departed " N-1 + Vintr
"The foolish boys climbed that shaky tower" becomes "boys climbed tower" N-1 + Vtr + N-3
"The old seeds found-in-the-barn produced many beautiful flowers" becomes "seeds produced flowers" N-1 + Vtr + N-3
"My youngest sister married George's nephew" becomes "sister married nephew" N-1 + Vtr + N-3
"Helen bought a blue woolen suit with-silver-buttons" becomes "Helen bought suit" N-1 + Vtr + N-3
Reminder-- A package, such as a phrase or a dependent clause, can act as a one-unit adjective.

Rule 3--Drop adverbs (unless they are predicate adverbs of time or place after a linking verb)

All words that tell When, Where, Why, How, How much, How often and How long are adverbs modifying verbs, adjectives or other adverbs.
They are dropped when we are looking for sentence pattern essentials.

"Some dogs always bark" becomes "Some dogs bark." ~ Now we apply rule 2 to get "dogs bark" N-I + Vintr
"My towel fell into-the-bathtub" becomes "My towel fell." Then we apply rule 2 to get "towel fell" N-1 + Vintr
"Maria screamed in-fright" becomes "Maria screamed" N-1 + Vintr
 "Joe talks softly when-the-baby-is-sleeping" becomes "Joe talks" N-1 + Vintr
"The little bell rang shrilly during-the-ceremony" becomes "The little bell rang" We then apply rule 2 to get "bell rang" N-1 + Vintr
"The children's festival continued until-sunset" becomes "The children's festival continued"
We then apply rule 2 to get "festival continued" N-1 + Vintr
Reminder--A package, such as a phrase or a dependent clause, can act as a one-unit adverb

Rule 4--Eliminate "not"

"That plant will not grow in sand" becomes "That plant will grow in sand."
We then keep applying necessary rules to strip the sentence down to its basic pattern. We apply rule 1 to get "That plant grow(s) in sand." (drop verb helpers)

We next apply rule 2 to get "plant grow(s) in sand" (drop noun servants) and rule 3 (drop adverbs) to get "plant grow(s) N-1 + Vintr "Plant grows" represents the basic sentence which had to undergo a series of changes (transformations) in order to become the final negative sentence. Our procedure in finding the sentence pattern will always take us to the basic sentence.

Rule 5--Discard editorial expressions

Editorial or transitional expressions are intrusions into the sentence. They are designed to help the reader follow or react to the message. In a series of sentences, they help the reader make a logical transition from one statement to the next. They have no grammatical function.

"Hopefully, our team will win" becomes "Our team will win"
We then apply rule1 to get "our team win(s)."
Next we apply rule 2 to get "team win(s)" N-1 + Vintr

"Of-course the audience applauded" becomes "the audience applauded" We then apply rule 2 to get "audience applauded "N-1+ Vintr

"On-the-other-hand, we must consider our budget" becomes "we must consider our budget"
We then apply rule 1 to get "we consider our budget"
We then apply rule 2 to get "we consider budget" N-1 + Vtr + N-3

Common editorial expressions include the following--
      at-any-rate
      consequently, hence, therefore
      first, second, third (never firstly, secondly, thirdly)
      for-example, for-instance
      furthermore, moreover
      hopefully, frankly
      however
      in-a-word, in-conclusion, to-conclude
      nevertheless
      on-the-other-hand

Repairing Sentences

Exercise 42

Some of the following sentences are structurally correct and some are either run-ons or fragments. Dissect each to uncover the sentence pattern(s). Is a necessary item missing? Are there two or more patterns put together without a connector? Correct the faulty sentences.

1. While the rain continued to flood the streets and the wind which had increased to gale force began to bring down some of the old trees
2. The students talked among themselves while the lecturer picked up the notes that he had dropped on the floor
3. The principal speaker at the political convention urged his supporters to ring doorbells and hand out leaflets although he knew that the Internet would play a major part in his campaign
4. Our town had too many snow days last winter the children had to go to school until the day before the Fourth of July
5. Hoping to win a college scholarship that would set him on the path to medical school Tom who had previously worked in his father's shop on weekends
6. When the railroad management decided that its trains would no longer stop at our town station the commuters had to find other ways of traveling to the city each day
7. When parents began taking their children to the new town pool for swimming lessons which were offered free for the first six months
8. Jennie explained that she had won the prize for the most delicious cheesecake by using a recipe which had been handed down in the family for several generations
9. Working with a new computer can be an exhausting experience the book of directions does not use language that the average person can understand
10. Nevertheless the detective did not realize that most of the youths who lived along the coast were excellent wind-surfers they could provide useful information about tides and currents although they were pretending to be ignorant.

Conflicts between Structure and Meaning

When simple sentences are combined into supersentences, the grammatical structures sometimes undercut the meaning. This is the cause of two kinds of problem sentences-- those with faulty parallelism and those with mis-subordination. Elimination of these errors is usually a simple matter of adjusting the connectors of the clauses and/or adding one or more missing words.

Faulty Parallelism

(I was hoping to find a place to park my car) but (no luck). Since "but" is a coordinate conjunction that must connect two grammatically equal items, it is obviously not doing its job in the sentence above. The second half of the sentence must be expanded into a clause that will match the structure of the opening clause.

Correction--I was hoping to find a place to park my car but (I had) no luck.
N-1 + Vtr + N-3 BUT N-1 + Vtr + N-3

Reminder--any kind of package can act as a sentence element. Here the infinitive phrase package ("to find a place to park my car") is acting as a noun (N3).

Mis-subordination

A stranger (who helped my grandmother cross the street) was wearing a green suit.

Here we have two full clauses which are joined grammatically, but the more important information has been put into a subordinate clause. The main clause-- "A stranger helped my grandmother cross the street"--should be the independent clause. Instead the use of the connector "who" demotes it to a subordinate clause acting like an adjective modifying "stranger." This means that (grammatically) it could be dropped, leaving "A stranger was wearing a green suit" as the main (most important) clause. This distorts the sentence message.

Correction--A stranger (who was wearing a green suit) helped my grandmother cross the street.
N-1 (N-1 + Vtr + N-3) +Vtr + N-3

Misuse of dependent clauses

As we have seen, supersentences often contain dependent clauses acting as nouns, adjectives or adverbs. These three kinds of clauses are not inter- changeable--a noun clause cannot be expected to do the job of an adjective; and an adjective or adverbial clause cannot be expected to do the job of a noun.

Careless choice of the connecting word, however, can lead to this kind of misuse.

Faulty--The reason for my lateness is (because my clock stopped)
Correct-The reason for my lateness is (that my clock stopped).

The faulty sentence contains a "why" connector ("because") which makes the clause into an adverb. However, the sentence pattern requires a noun telling us "what," not "why."(N-1 + link verb + Nn-1) "That" is a conjunction which can be the connector for a noun clause.

Faulty--My favorite time of day is (when my children are in school)
Correct--My favorite time of day is the interval (when my children are in school).

Again, the faulty sentence is using an adverbial clause ("when") as an Nn-1. By adding the noun "interval," we supply the needed Nn-1 and change the dependent clause into an adjective modifying "interval."

> Faulty--The fugitive's hiding place was (where he had discovered a cave).
> Correct--The fugitive's hiding place was a spot (where he had discovered a cave).

This time the connector in the faulty sentence is telling "where" and thus introducing an adverbial clause where an Nn-1 is needed. It is a simple matter to supply a noun ("spot") and let the dependent clause act as an adjective.

Summary-- avoid using the expressions "is because, is when, is where."

Exercise 43

Some of the sentences below are run-ons or fragments. Others contain faulty parallelism or mis-subordination. Label the problem in each incorrect sentence and make the necessary correction. (Punctuation has been omitted.)

1. A hurricane forced the cruise ship scheduled to sail to South America to remain in its Florida port for three extra days this created serious scheduling problems
2. The strenuous sport of sky-diving has become very popular but not with older people
3. Tom and Walter bought a lottery ticket together although Walter was uneasy about gambling
4. When we arrived at our hotel we took a short walk before dinner it was a bad decision because we lost our way
5. The monkey who snatched tourists' sunglasses is named Chippie
6. The painting which had been stolen from the museum and recently recovered was considered a masterpiece
7. The van was a new GM model that ran up on the sidewalk and smashed the store window
8. The young boys who came to the golf course every summer morning to search for lost balls which they planned to sell
9. The council member opposed the new tax and that it would not solve the budget problem
10. The children who took a bus to the summer day camp located on a lake about ten miles from their town

CHAPTER 8

EXPLORING SENTENCE VARIETY

Sentence Length, Movability of Sentence Parts, Orchestration of Sentences in a Paragraph

Sentence Length

Sometimes we want to make our sentences less wordy so they can be read more rapidly. On the other hand, a paragraph composed solely of short direct sentences has a staccato effect that can convey a sense of urgency even when there is no need for it A skillful writer (or speaker) suits his style to the requirements of the moment. He is aware of occasions when longer, more leisurely sentences would be more appropriate than short ones. Above all, he knows that clarity should never be sacrificed for brevity. It is important, therefore, to learn how to vary our sentences and how to orchestrate them when writing paragraphs. The ability to do this comes with practice.

Long to Short

1. The dancer (who is wearing satin toe shoes) is the star of the show.
2. The dancer (wearing satin toe shoes) is the star of the show.
3. The dancer (in satin toe shoes) is the star of the show.

We have reduced a dependent clause to a verbal adjective phrase and then to a prepositional phrase.

1. A building (which has six sides) can become a tourist attraction.
2. A building (with six sides) can become a tourist attraction.
3. A (six-sided) building can become a tourist attraction.

We reduced the dependent clause to a prepositional phrase and then to a compound adjective. Notice the use of the hyphen-- which makes this kind of adjective possible and the placement of the adjective in front of the noun.

In the preceding set of sentences, we cannot use the hyphen device—

"The satin-toe-shoed dancer" is too clumsy because it is too long.

> 1. The girl (who had curly hair) won the beauty contest.
> 2. The girl (with curly hair) won the beauty contest
> 3. The (curly-haired) girl won the beauty contest.

> 1. (After the dessert was served), the speeches began.
> 2. (After the dessert), the speeches began.

Sometimes it's possible to delete a word or two without affecting the meaning.

> 1. The children did not complain, (although dinner was late).
> 2. (Although dinner was late), the children did not complain.
> 3. The children did not complain (about the late dinner).

There is no difference between sentences #1 and #2 except that the writer of the first preferred one sequence and the writer of the second preferred the other. Both are correct. However, when the dependent clause is reduced to a prepositional phrase, that phrase should come after the verb. "About the late dinner the children did not complain" is grammatically correct but awkward, as though the writer was straining for a literary effect. Notice that the prepositional phrase is made of up the two important words in the dependent clause ("late dinner") plus the preposition "about."

Short to Long

> 1. The fans started leaving (before the game ended).
> 2. The fans started leaving (before the end of the game).

Here the dependent clause was changed into a compound prepositional phrase (one large phrase containing a smaller phrase) making the sentence a trifle longer. The difference in length is so slight that nothing is gained or lost. It is simply a matter of which version the writer prefers. When two whole sentences are combined into one, the change is more significant. The resulting supersentence acquires more weight.

As we saw in Chapter 4 (Major League Word Packages), there are two kinds of combined sentences—those that link equally important ideas and those that link unequally important ideas. In a supersentence with equally important ideas, no judgment needs to be made.

> 1. (You take the high road) + (I'll take the low road)
> 2. (I'll take the low road)+ (You take the high road).

The connector "and" guarantees the equality (as would "or," "nor," "but," or a semicolon).
However, if we wish to emphasize one idea at the expense of the other, we choose a connector that makes this possible.

      3. If (you take the high road), (I'll take the low road).

The subordinate conjunction "if" demotes the clause "you take the high road" to a less important status.

A thoughtful writer is careful to choose the right kind of connector to convey his meaning.

      1. Jack crossed the finish line first and he won the gold medal.

Here we have two clauses joined by the connector "and," which denies the cause-and-effect relationship between the two statements.

      2. Because Jack crossed the finish line first, he won the gold medal.

The subordinate conjunction "because" makes the whole sentence more meaningful by indicating the cause-and-effect relationship.

      3. Having crossed the finish line first, Jack won the gold medal.

Here we have an alternate way of indicating the cause-and-effect relationship--the use of the verbal phrase "Having crossed the finish line first" instead of the subordinate clause "Because he crossed the finish line first."
This method of showing the cause-and-effect relationship reduces the subordinate idea from a clause to a phrase and relies on the difference in tenses. "Having crossed" indicates that this action preceded "won." This shortens the supersentence while still conveying the same message. The choice between a shorter and a longer sentence is a matter of the writer's preference.

Movability of Sentence Parts

As we saw in some of the preceding sentence conversions, some elements can be moved from one end of the sentence to the other, and some elements cannot be moved. The principal movable items are adverbial, although as we shall see, occasional adjectival movement is possible.

In a basic sentence, the subject noun (N-1) comes first. After the subject (with all its possible modifiers) has been mentioned, we cross an invisible line and enter the predicate area of the sentence. This area runs to the end of the sentence. Its one essential element is the verb. In many cases there may be an additional essential element-- the verb complement (N-2, N-3, Nn-1, Nn-3, Pred. Adj, Pred. Adv). In addition there may be minor elements such as verb helpers and verb modifiers (adverbs). All of these, normally, are on the right side of the invisible line separating subject and predicate, and all of them occupy a specific place in the sentence sequence. However, in unusual situations where the writer wishes to emphasize a particular element in the predicate, he might put it at the beginning of the sentence.

> 1. Normal order--The scientist brought his experiment to a close (step by careful step).
> 2. Adverbial movement--(Step by careful step), the scientist brought his experiment to a close.

Here the writer wanted to emphasize the meticulous work of the scientist and so he moved this adverbial cluster from the end of the sentence to the beginning.

A displacement like this can be very effective, but should be used in moderation.

Adjectival Movement

By and large, adjectives belong next to the nouns they modify and cannot be picked up and moved elsewhere in the sentence. However there are two exceptions to this rule.

Generally adjective packages follow the noun and single-word adjectives precede the noun. Once in a while--not too often--the "single-word" adjective turns out to be two words made into a single word by the use of a hyphen.

> 1. Normal position for an adjective clause--The baby (who has blue eyes) is my niece.
> 2. Normal position for an adjective phrase--The baby (with blue eyes) is my niece.
> 3. Unusual position-- The (blue-eyed) baby is my niece.

The clause/phrase has been collapsed into a hyphenated adjective which is considered to be a single word.

A more common adjectival movement occurs with verbal adjective phrases.

> 1. The speaker (waving his arms wildly) amused the audience.
> 2. (Waving his arms wildly) the speaker amused the audience.

While each of these adjectival phrases occupies a different position, the fact remains that each is next to the noun it modifies. This is the general adjective-noun position.

Adverbial Movement

Although adverbs and adverb packages are generally movable, there are bound to be some exceptions. This happens because there are many different kinds of adverbs. (See Chapter 2.)

"Only" is a slippery adverb that is frequently misused. It should immediately precede the word it modifies.

> Only I can understand you. (No one else can.)
> I can only listen to you. (I cannot help you.)
> We invited only a few of our friends. (We did not invite many.)
> The scouts were only half way home. (Not close)

Anything at the start or end of the sentence stands out. The writer chooses the position according to the effect he wants to create. The question of what sounds like English and what does not comes down to the matter of idiom. The ear of the native speaker (or writer) tells him what sounds right. The newcomer to English can develop this facility by continual reading and listening.

Exercise 44
Variations in Sentence Openings

Identify the grammatical unit or structures that precede the subject in each of the following sentences.

Note--In a whole paragraph, such a series of unusual sentence openings would be undesirable. We are all conditioned to expect the subject to come first, and the necessity of adjusting again and again to an unusual beginning would become a strain. (Punctuation has been omitted.)

1. Silently the contestants waited on the sidelines to hear the judge's decision.
2. In the packed gymnasium the weary contestants waited to hear the judge announce the winner.
3. Flushed and weary young people the contestants waited silently to hear the judge announce the winner.
4. To hear the judge announce the winner the contestants waited silently on the sidelines.
5. Waiting silently the weary contestants expected the judge's decision.
6. As if they had abandoned all hope of winning the weary contestants waited silently on the sidelines.
7. With high hopes the contestants waited in the packed gymnasium to hear the decision of the judge.
8. In the packed gymnasium seated before the judges the weary contestants waited to hear the decision.
9. Sitting silently and smiling nervously the contestants waited for the decision.

10. To hear the judges announce the decision and to find out what the winning point score was the contestants waited silently on the sidelines.
11. Silently nervously expectantly the contestants in the packed gymnasium awaited the decision.
12. In the packed gymnasium across from the judges directly below a cluster of flags the contestants sat waiting to hear the decision.
13. Heads up faces tense eyes bright the contestants waited silently.
14. Silently eyes bright with excitement the contestants waited on the sidelines.
15. While they waited to hear the name of the winner the contestants sat silently.

The choice of the most effective among several versions of a sentence depends as much on the writer's "ear" as it does on his desire to highlight a particular detail. Which of the preceding sentences seem to be particularly effective in terms of their opening? Which openings strike you as too long? too wordy?

Exercise 45
Variations in Sentence Closings

Examine the second half of the sentence. Is it a normal predicate consisting of the verb plus or minus an adverb or a complement such as an object or predicate noun? If not, what grammatical unit or structure ends the sentence? Where there is such a unit or structure, does it, or do they, make the sentence more effective (favorable) or overdone (unfavorable)? (Bear in mind the fact that material at the very end of the sentence is in a spotlight position.) (Punctuation has been omitted.)

1. The contestants were silent an attractive group of young people waiting to hear the decision.
2. Five figures silent and tense sat on the sidelines in the packed gymnasium.
3. The contestants tense but cheerful awaited the decision.
4. The contestants were attractive figures slimmed by exercise disciplined by practice and bright-eyed with anticipation.
5. The contestants who had been training for months sat with their coaches waiting to hear the decision.
6. The contestants their eyes fixed on the judges waited expectantly for the decision.
7. The contestants waiting for the decision gazed expectantly at the judges.
8. The contestants in the aftermath of their precise and beautiful routines waited for the judges to announce the decision.

9. The contestants sat silent not only to hear the decision but also to demonstrate that they were disciplined athletes.
10. The contestants sat as if they were ready for anything as if all their training had not been leading up to this moment.

Exercise 46
Interrupters of the Sentence Flow

In the sentences above (Exercise 45), find the interrupters, if any, of the subject-verb-complement flow and identify them grammatically. We are looking for word packages such as clauses, phrases, clusters, and pair/series. We are not looking for single adjectives or adverbs.

      Example--The city's tax rate attracted many new businessmen.
          rate attracted businessmen--no interrupter
      Example--The city's tax rate (which had climbed recently) discouraged new business.
          rate discouraged business (interrupted by adjective clause modifying "rate")
      Example--The city's tax rate attracted businesses struggling to appeal to young people.
          rate attracted businesses--no interrupter

The verbal adjective phrase "struggling to appeal to young people" modifies "businesses," but does not interrupt the N-1 + action verb + N-3 sequence of the sentence.

Exercise 47
Reversals

A writer will sometimes change the normal subject-verb-complement order of a sentence pattern to achieve variety or to emphasize a particular detail by putting it at the beginning. This kind of reversal (of sentence pattern elements) should be used sparingly.

Analyze the following sentences to see what the writer has done to the sentence pattern. Would any of these sentences be more effective in normal word order?

1. The strain of continuing success in a competitive field he knew all too well.
2. Less changeable than a garden of mixed flowers is an expanse of lawn bordered by evergreen shrubs.
3. Hard as steel he was in the face of hostile criticism.
4. Fortunate are those people who early in life learn the importance of saving.
5. Sure to be signed again by the film producer, the new star had to fight off a horde of reporters and photographers.

Supersentences

Although we have been discussing single sentence patterns and the joining of two patterns in various ways, the fact is that writing—particularly writing intended for print—is more complicated, Joining three or four patterns in varying degrees of subordination to produce an intricate supersentence is common. The best writing is a mixture of sentence structures. How this mixture is achieved depends upon the writer.

Exercise 48

How many sentence patterns are joined in each of the following supersentences?
(Clue—how many main verbs are there?)
Which patterns are independent clauses and which are dependent clauses?
(Clue—locate the connectors. Those which do not introduce dependent clauses are "and, but, or, nor.")
Do any of these supersentences strike you as too complicated in terms of structure? (Punctuation has been omitted.)

1. Our guide decided that as long as the weather remained favorable we would continue our climb to the summit where we could remain overnight.
2. Tom and his young nephew were going to the museum to see the mummies but when the boy received a computer game for his birthday he decided to stay home and play it.
3. When the comedian went backstage to remove his makeup after the show ended he found his dressing room filled with people who wanted his autograph because he had become famous.
4. The boat which we had boarded at dawn chugged slowly up the river until we reached a little village where we went ashore for an early lunch.
5. Since the new reporter who had been assigned to interview the mayor did not even know where city hall was located he telephoned the mayor's secretary whom he had met a few days before.
6. Before radio was invented people who had old-fashioned alarm clocks would sometimes be late for work if they forgot to wind them at bedtime.
7. It was late autumn and the weatherman had predicted a possible snowstorm that would block some of the high-altitude roads but my cousin's family still planned to drive straight through the mountains to California.

8. William expected to get a Christmas bonus unless his company unexpectedly lost the contract that was coming up for renewal before the holidays began.
9. Because Joe Smith's heating bills had been increasing every year he finally said to his wife that they should move to a smaller house which would help them stay within the budget that they had worked out when their son needed money for his college tuition.
10. Whenever Nancy took her children to the beach she had to take along little Jennie's three stuffed animals and Baby Eddie's sand pail with two shovels while she juggled the lunch basket and towels and the beach bag containing all the swimsuits.

For our practical purposes, effective writing consists of sentences that are neither too complicated nor too simple. It is wise to assume that our reader will be someone who is in a hurry but who still wants the respect that careful writing implies.

Orchestration of Sentences in the Paragraph

Use variety in moderation for sentence openings and closings.
Use a mixture of simple and supersentences.
Occasionally use a rhetorical question.
Include examples and brief descriptive detail to relieve density.

Since the function of everyday writing is efficient communication, the reader's attention should never be drawn away from the message. Monotonous sequences of subject-verb-complement can cause his attention to wander. Too many long complicated sentences can slow down his reading. Too many short simple sentences can sound didactic.

On the other hand, overdoing variety can be self-defeating. In general, sentences which state basic facts or arguments should be reasonably simple and straightforward without a tangle of dependent clauses. Details and examples can be presented in sentences with more grammatical complications because details have immediate interest. In an article, report, or explanation consisting of more than one paragraph, a question or two can relieve the onward march of flat statements. There are no rules or formulas, but one bit of advice may be useful—when in doubt, keep it simple.

A FEW NOTES ON WRITING

It has been said that television and popular culture have shortened everyone's attention span to the extent that we are unwilling to stay with one subject very long. Whether or not this is true, it is a fact that the modern craze for speed makes it unlikely that most readers will linger over a page in order to admire the style or consider the implications of what is being stated.

All of this puts pressure on writers to be quick and clear. A sentence can no longer have the many dependent clauses found in the stately long-winded writing of the old-fashioned prose masters. Nowadays overloaded sentences strain our patience and the careful writer avoids them.

Modern English avoids rhetorical flourishes, overuse of figurative language, and indulgence in alliteration. Mythological or Biblical allusions or quotations from Shakespeare nowadays would mark our writing as old-fashioned. Americans react negatively to flowery language, and they are not impressed by a show of learning. In addition, most fancy writing will be wasted on the modern reader, whose education has often stressed the practical at the expense of the cultural. Although an established professional writer may become known for his special style, it is advisable for the rest of us to stick to plain writing.

On the other hand, our writing should show that we did give it some thought. This means that we delete repetition (as in "the modern world of today") and clichés (wornout expressions, such as "this moment in time").

The desire to include humor or noticeable originality in utilitarian writing should be evaluated in terms of the prospective reader. A harried businessman is not the ideal audience. Resist the temptation to be "hip" unless you are in the entertainment or sports world.

Despite the increasing informal—even slangy—use of spoken English in the United States, it is advisable to be conservative in written English. Written material has a way of turning up in inappropriate circumstances long after it was composed. In business and the professions, the tone (as in "tone of voice") of one's writing can be important.

Tone can be established in a number of ways, but mostly by the choice of vocabulary and the construction of sentences. Polysyllabic Latinate words in long ponderous sentences represent a conservative extreme that has largely been abandoned, except for some legal documents. Breezy short sentences full of current popular expressions go to the other extreme. The best choice lies in the middle.

Pronoun use can play a part in establishing tone. For example, the pronoun "one" is rarely used in the U.S. In Britain we might find the sentence "One must prepare carefully for one's retirement." In this country we would write (or say) "We must prepare carefully for our retirement" or "You should prepare carefully for your retirement." (The use of "you" and "your," however, can create too much of a preachy tone for readers to tolerate.)

The pronoun "I" presents another problem which is best avoided by writing in the third person. When first-person use is necessary, as in a letter of application, it may take some ingenuity to keep "I" to a minimum. "Myself" cannot be used as a substitute. ("My former employer and myself believed...") This is a misuse of "myself" which can only be used together with "I." Although most advertising is based upon bragging about a company or product, bragging about oneself brings nothing but disapproval. Despite the revelations that clutter up television and the popular press, serious people are expected to be reticent about their personal lives and modest about their accomplishments.

Contemporary stress on gender equality has led to awkwardness in the use of "his" and "her." The masculine pronoun used to be the norm--"A person should prepare carefully for his retirement." Then it became "A person should prepare carefully for his or her retirement." This double pronoun use has proved too clumsy for most writers, many of whom now alternately use "his" and "her" throughout a lengthy piece.

In spoken English the gender equality dilemma is avoided by the cheerful use of a grammatical error—"A person should prepare carefully for their retirement." This use of a plural ("their") to refer for a singular noun ("person") is still taught as an error. (A pronoun is supposed to agree with its antecedent in gender and number.) Nevertheless, in the world outside of the classroom, this use of "their" is the general solution for what to do about being fair to both masculine and feminine.

In spoken English we have a problem with the answer to the question "Who is it?" A traditional grammar textbook would insist on the answer "It is I." However, that is too pedantic. Almost everyone would answer, "It's me."

Some Contemporary Usages To Avoid

1. Insertion of "of" into certain expressions

It was not that big of a deal—wrong.
It was not that big a deal--correct

The worker fell off of the roof—wrong.
The worker fell off the roof--correct

However, we do use "of" after "much," "most," and "many."

Much of the money had been wasted—correct
My little brother ate most of the cake—correct
Many of the spectators grumbled about the referee's decisions—correct

2. Insertion of "up" as an intensifier

The intruder was beaten up by the homeowner—wrong.
The intruder was beaten by the homeowner—correct
The sales clerk wrapped up my purchase—wrong
The sales clerk wrapped my purchase—correct

3. Omission of key word or words

I could care less—wrong
I couldn't care less—correct
I know to carry my driver's license—wrong
I know enough to carry my driver's license—correct
I like that the prices of houses are coming down"—wrong
I like the fact that the prices of houses are coming down"— correct

4. Confusion of "all right" and "already"

"Already" is a time-indicating word.

I hurried to the station, but the train had already left.
The ocean level is rising. Some seacoast is already under water.

"All right" has three meanings--

a) adjective meaning "healthy"--
Ed was sick yesterday, but he's all right today.
b) response indicating agreement--
All right. I'll lend you my watch.
c) two separate words, each a separate part of speech--
All my students got the test answers right.
My students got all the test answers right.

When two words have a superficial resemblance, look at them carefully. Notice the difference between them and use them accordingly.

126

GLOSSARY

abstract noun—a noun that refers to something intangible (See "concrete noun.")

action verb--a verb that names an action

active voice—the normal form of a transitive verb in a sentence whereby the doer of the action—the subject (N-1)—appears to the left of the verb and the receiver of the action—the object (N-3) follows the verb

adjective--a word that describes a noun

adjective clause--a subject-verb construction that describes a noun

adjective cluster—a grammatical unit consisting of an adjective (head word) with one or more modifiers

adverb--a word that tells something about the verb or which modifies an adjective or another adverb

adverb clause--a subject-verb construction that tells something about the verb or which modifies an adjective or another adverb

adverb cluster—a grammatical unit consisting of an adverb (head word) with one or more modifiers

antecedent—a noun mentioned earlier in the sentence as the reference point for a pronoun that comes later

apostrophe (')—a mark used in combination with "s" on a noun to indicate possession. When used in other words, it signals that a letter has been omitted.

appositive--a noun that stands next to another noun with the same meaning in order to give additional information

article—a pre-noun modifier, either definite ("the") or indefinite ("a, an") in meaning

auxiliary—a helping verb preceding the main verb in order to form a compound tense or to form the negative or to ask a question or to form the passive voice or to shade the verb's meaning (See "shading.")

basic sentence—a sentence stripped of all but its essentials-- subject word, main verb, and complement (if any)

buried question--an indirect question

case—a classification of pronoun forms into nominative, possessive, or objective case depending upon their use in a sentence. "Case" does not refer to nouns except when they are spelled with an apostrophe plus "s" to show ownership. They are then said to be in the possessive case.

clause—a sentence pattern that can stand alone (independent clause) or a pattern that cannot stand alone (dependent clause) because it has been weakened by the addition of a subordinating connector

cluster—a grammatical unit consisting of a head word (noun, verb, adjective or adverb) plus modifiers and/or auxiliaries and/or complements

collective noun--a noun referring to a group of similar members

common noun--a noun referring to a non-specific group (See "proper noun.")

complement—a noun, pronoun, adjective, or adverb that completes the meaning of the verb by acting as object (N-3), indirect object (N-2), predicate noun, predicate pronoun, predicate adjective, or predicate adverb of time or place

concrete noun—a noun that names a physical or material thing (See "abstract noun.")

conjugation---a chart showing all forms of a particular verb, taking it through all tenses in the singular and plural and in first, second, and third persons. All these forms are shown in the indicative, subjunctive, imperative, and progressive modes.

conjunction--a word that connects

connector (known in traditional grammar as a "conjunction")—one of a limited number of words which join two or more units. It creates grammatical equality or inequality by means of its semantic nature. The connector may be a coordinator, a subordinator, a relator, or an interrogator.

contraction—the shortening of a word by omitting a letter and substituting an apostrophe, as in "isn't" for "is not."

coordinator/coordinate conjunction—one of a limited number of connectors for grammatical units that are considered of equal importance (See "subordinator.")

count noun—a noun referring to something specific that can be counted (See "mass noun.")

dangling participle—a grammatical error in a sentence caused by putting a participle (verbal adjective) or participial (verbal adjective) phrase next to a noun it does not modify

declarative sentence—a sentence that makes a statement

demonstrative adjective—"this, that, these, those"—any of these words used as adjectives to point out their nouns

demonstrative pronoun—"this, that, these, those"—any of these pointing-out words used to refer to previously mentioned noun or nouns.

dependent clause—a sentence pattern which cannot stand alone because of the addition of a subordinating, a relating, or an interrogating connector.

determiner—a pre-noun modifier, such as an article, possessive noun or pronoun, quantifier, demonstrative adjective

direct object (N-3)—a noun or pronoun which follows an action verb and is the receiver of the action

direct question—an inquiry introduced either by a "WH-" word or by the use of an auxiliary preceding the subject. It is punctuated with a question mark. (See "indirect question" and "tag question.")

emphatic form of the verb—the use of any form of "do" with a main verb to indicate emphasis

empty "it"—when used as the subject of a sentence about weather or time, "it" has no meaning. e.g. "It is cold." "It is four o'clock."

exclamatory sentence—a sentence that is an exclamation, usually showing emotion. It is punctuated with an exclamation mark.

expletive—subject (N-1) place holder ("it" or "there")

free-lance word--a word that serves no grammatical function

gender—classification of personal pronouns (in the singular only) as masculine, feminine, or neuter, depending upon the gender of the noun referred to-- "he, his, him, she, her, hers, it, its."   English uses natural gender, except for the tendency to refer to nature, boats, and some countries as feminine and to refer to animals as neuter when their sex is unknown.

genitive—the name of a case in Latin occasionally borrowed to describe a noun possessive that uses an "of" phrase instead of apostrophe plus "s." ("the tail of the dog" instead of "the dog's tail")

gerund—a verbal noun that is formed by adding "-ing" to the basic form of a verb. This manual uses the term "verbal noun."

gerund phrase—a grammatical unit used as a noun. It consists of a gerund with modifiers and/or complements. This manual uses the term "verbal noun phrase."

head word—a noun, verb, adjective, or adverb with modifiers and/or complements forming the grammatical unit known as a cluster.

helping verb—(see also "auxiliary")—a verb which precedes the main verb in a sentence pattern and which does the job of indicating tense, mood, passive voice, emphasis, negation, or continuing action.

imperative mood--the aspect of the verb in a sentence giving a command

imperative sentence--a sentence giving a command

independent clause--a sentence pattern, also known as a simple sentence

 indicative—the form of the verb in a sentence pattern that is not interrogative, imperative, or exclamatory. Such sentences are said to be declarative.

indicative mood--the aspect of a verb in a sentence indicating that it is a statement of fact

indirect object (N-2)—a noun or pronoun appearing immediately after the verb and preceding the direct object (N-3). It never appears without a direct object. The indirect object refers to the person or thing affected by the action of the verb.

indirect question—an embedded sentence pattern introduced by a question word ("WH-" or "HOW") This embedded pattern follows a verb of inquiry such as "asked, inquired, wondered." (See "direct question" and "tag question.")

infinitive—a verb preceded by "to." It is used as a noun, an adjective, or adverb.

infinitive phrase—a grammatical unit used as a noun, adjective, or adverb. It consists of an infinitive with any of the following: a subject noun or pronoun, auxiliaries, modifiers, complements. Essentially a telescoped dependent clause, it is sometimes introduced by "for."

interrogative adjective--a WH- word that modifies a noun in a direct or indirect question

interrogative adverb--a WH- word or HOW which modifies a verb, an adjective or another adverb in a direct or indirect question

interrogative pronoun--a WH- word ("who, whom, what") used in a noun position in a direct or indirect question

interrogative sentence--a sentence that asks a question

interrogator—a word that asks a question (a WH- word or How) in combination with a question mark or a questioning verb such as "asked, inquired, wondered."

intransitive—a verb classification—used to describe a sentence pattern verb not followed by a direct object (See "transitive.")

linking (link) verb—a non-action verb. It will be followed by a predicate noun (Nn-1), a predicate adjective, or a predicate adverb of time or place. "Be" is the most common linking verb.

mass noun—a noun which refers to something not countable , therefore neither singular nor plural

modal—a type of helping verb used to shade the meaning of the main verb (See "shading.")

132

mood (also spelled "mode")--the aspect of the main verb in a sentence that tells how the sentence message is to be regarded--as a command, as an emotional outburst, as a wish or doubt, or as a statement of fact

N-1--the subject word in a sentence pattern

N-2--the indirect object in a sentence pattern after a transitive verb. It must always be followed by a direct object (N-3).

N-3--the direct object after a transitive verb. It may or may not be preceded by an indirect object.

Nn-1--a noun following a link verb that renames the subject noun.

Nn-3--a noun following a direct object. It renames the object. It is traditionally called "objective complement," meaning "completer of the object."

negator—an adverb ("not" or "never") that makes a sentence pattern negative

nominative case—a term borrowed from Latin to describe a pronoun form when it is acting as subject (N-1) or predicate noun (Nn-1). (See "possessive" and "objective.")

noun—a word referring to a person, place, thing, idea, possibility, occurrence, or condition

noun adjunct—a noun used as a pre-nominal modifier of another noun

noun clause--a subject-verb construction that does a noun job in a sentence

noun cluster—a grammatical unit used as a noun It consists of a noun head word with modifiers.

object of a preposition--a noun or pronoun that follows a preposition to form the grammatical unit called a prepositional phrase

objective case—a classification for a pronoun acting as the direct or indirect object of a verb or as the object of a preposition. (See "nominative" and "possessive.")

objective complement (Nn-3)—a noun immediately following a direct object (N-3) in a sentence pattern. It renames or specifies the direct object noun.

overloaded sentence—1) a simple sentence pattern with too many modifying phrases or too many adjectives or adverbs.

2) a supersentence with too many embedded dependent clauses

pair/series—1) pair—a grammatical unit consisting of two nouns, adjectives, adverbs, verbs, or grammatical units connected by "and," "but," "or," or "nor"

2) series—a grammatical unit similar to (1)except that it consists or three or more similar elements

participial phrase—a grammatical unit consisting of a participle with any or all of the following: modifiers, auxiliaries, complements. This manual uses the term "verbal adjective phrase."

participle--a verb form acting as an adjective. This manual uses the term "verbal adjective."

particle—a short word following a verb that intensifies or changes the meaning of the verb

passive voice—a transformation of an action verb in a sentence pattern so that the object (receiver of the action) occupies the subject position and the true subject (doer of the action) appears after the verb as the object of the preposition "by." (See "active voice.") .

person—a classification of personal pronouns into those which refer to the speaker or speakers ("I, my, mine, me, we, us, our, ours") as first person; those which refer to the person or persons spoken to ("you, your, yours"), as second person, and those which refer to the person or persons spoken about ("he, his, him, she, her, hers, her, it, its, they, their, their, them") as third person.

phrase—a grammatical unit acting as a noun, an adjective, or adverb. Depending upon its key word, it is a prepositional phrase, a verbal noun phrase, a verbal adjective phrase, or an infinitive phrase. In addition to its key word, it contains any or all of the following: complement, auxiliaries, modifiers.

place holder—either "it" or "there" can occupy the subject position (N-1) in a sentence pattern so that the true subject (usually a phrase or a dependent clause) can follow the verb.

possessive case-- classification of a pronoun or noun form that indicates connection or ownership (See "nominative" and "objective.")

post-noun modifier—any multi-word unit that follows the noun it modifies

predicate--the second half of a sentence pattern. A predicate must contain a verb with or without a complement. A predicate with an intransitive verb needs nothing more. A predicate with a transitive verb must contain one of the following--N-3, N-2 + N-3, or N-3 + Nn-3. A predicate with a link verb must be contain one of the following--Nn-1, predicate pronoun, predicate adjective, or predicate adverb of place or time.

predicate adjective—an adjective that follows a linking verb, acting as its complement and describing the subject .

predicate adverb of time or place—an adverb that follows a linking verb, acting as its complement and describing the subject noun in terms of location or time

predicate noun or pronoun—a noun or pronoun (Nn-1) that follows a linking verb, acting as its complement and renaming the subject noun

pre-noun modifier--any one-word modifier that precedes the noun.

preposition—a word that tells direction, location, connection, or time and which, in combination with a noun or pronoun, forms a prepositional phrase. A preposition never appears alone.

progressive verb—a form of the verb showing continued action. It is formed by the addition of "-ing" to the main verb and the placing of a correct form of the auxiliary "be" in front of it.

pronoun—a word that replaces a noun in a sentence or a series of sentences so that the noun does not have to be repeated

proper noun—a noun, always capitalized, that refers to a particular member of a class or group (See "common noun.")

quantifier—a pre-noun modifier indicating how many, either definitely, such as "three" or indefinitely, such as "some"

referent—the item in the real world that a noun or pronoun names relative adjective—a connector which attaches a dependent clause to the independent clause in a sentence and which also acts as an adjective in its own clause

relative adverb—a connector which attaches a dependent clause to the independent clause in a sentence and which also acts as an adverb in its own clause

relative clause—one kind of dependent clause which is headed by a relative adjective, relative adverb, or relative pronoun (See "subordinate clause.")

relative pronoun—a connector which attaches a dependent clause to the independent clause in a sentence and which also acts as a pronoun in its own clause

relator--an adjective, adverb or pronoun that connects a dependent clause to the independent clause and also acts as an adjective, adverb or pronoun in its own clause

restricter—a word narrowing the focus of the word or word group that follows. Common restricters include "especially, even, just, merely, only, particularly."

rhetorical question—a question used chiefly for effect. No answer is expected.

sentence pattern—the arrangement of basic elements in a clause— always a subject and a verb and sometimes a complement. The clause can be dependent or independent.

shading the meaning of the verb—the addition of a particular helper which indicates one of the following—ability ("can, could"), chance ("may, might"), courage ("dare"), customary action ("will, would"), determination ("will, would"), emphasis ("do, did"), necessity ("must, have to, had to"), obligation ("ought, should,"), permission ("may, might"), possibility (" can, could"), probability ("may, might")

simple sentence--a subject-verb combination that can stand alone grammatically. (See "independent clause.")

split infinitive—the insertion of an adverb between "to" and the verb

subject (N-1)—the noun or pronoun that precedes the verb in a sentence pattern written in normal word order. It names the person or thing that the verb is referring to.

subjunctive mood--the aspect of the main verb in a sentence indicating that the message is expressing doubt, a wish, or an impossibility

subordinate clause—a kind of dependent clause which consists of a complete sentence pattern preceded by a subordinate conjunction (See "relative clause.")

subordinate conjunction—a connector of a dependent clause to the independent clause. It plays no grammatical role other than to connect. (See "coordinator.")

subordinator--alternate term for "subordinate conjunction"

supersentence—a sentence consisting of more than one clause. It must contain at least one independent clause.

tag question—a negative or affirmative short query which, when added to the end of a statement, makes it interrogative (See "direct question" and "indirect question.")

transitive—the description of a verb that transfers the action of the subject (N-1) to the direct object (N-3). (See "intransitive.")

verb cluster—a grammatical unit consisting of a verb (head word) with any or all of the following—auxiliary, modifiers, complements

verbal adjective--a verb form that acts like an adjective

verbal noun--a verb form that acts like a noun

Vintr--intransitive verb--It does not transfer action..

Vlink--linking verb--a non-action verb that forms an equation. Its complement always renames, describes, or locates the subject in space or time.

voice--the two possibilities for a transitive (action) verb in a sentence pattern. (See "active voice" and "passive voice.")

Vtr--a verb that transfers action to the direct object (N-3)

"WH-" word—"what, when, where, which, who, whose, whom, why" "How" is also a member of this group.

" WH- Club"--the "wh-" words and "how"

yes/no question—a query to which the expected answer is "Yes," "No" or "Maybe" It is in contrast with a request for information.

138

APPENDIX A

CHAPTER 1

Noun Forms--categories, singular/plural
Pronoun Forms and Uses
Verbs--principal parts, tenses, moods, 6 verb functions

Nouns

There are two classes of nouns--proper and common. A proper noun refers to a particular person, place, or thing, and it is always capitalized--

London, Atlantic, Shakespeare, Thanksgiving, Harvard
A common noun refers to a member of a general class --

city, ocean, playwright, holiday, university
It is not capitalized.
An adjective which is derived from a proper noun is also capitalized--

America--proper noun, American--proper adjective.

Other ways of classifying nouns refer to different aspects of their meaning--
1. count vs. mass nouns
A count noun is one that belongs to a class of things that can be counted--

tie, car, storm
A mass noun belongs to a class of things that name generalities. They cannot be counted—

fuel, patriotism, beauty, mist
A count noun has a plural form and can take a plural verb. A mass noun does not have a plural form and always takes a singular verb.

count--Dad borrowed my new tie and ruined it. He
already owes me two new ties.
mass--Fuel is going to be scarce.
Some nouns can be either count or mass depending on the meaning of the sentence in which they appear.

count--A cup of coffee is always welcome. Two cups of
coffee are doubly welcome.
mass--Coffee is often forbidden to children.

2. abstract vs. concrete nouns

An abstract noun usually refers to a quality or state. A concrete noun refers to a physical or material person, place, or thing.

> abstract--The pilgrim sought peace.
> concrete--The pilgrim carried a book.

3. collective nouns

A collective noun refers to a group which acts as a single unit and therefore requires a singular verb. Only a few nouns are used this way--

> "committee, class, council, crew, group, jury" are the most common.
> collective--The committee is ready to publish its report.

No matter where a noun occurs in a sentence, it remains an element whose form can change only for 2 reasons--

1. to indicate number (singular or plural)
2. to indicate ownership (possessive case)

Singular or plural--

We add "-s" to a base noun--"river/rivers"-- to indicate plural unless it ends in "s, x, z, ch, sh." In these cases we add "-es"--dress/dresses, fox/foxes, buzz/buzzes, church/churches, dish/dishes.

Since there are many exceptions to the rules for pluralizing, the use of a dictionary is advised.

Note—Whether a noun is singular or plural, count or non-count, common or proper makes no difference in its sentence job. It will act as a subject, object of the verb, objective complement, object of a preposition, or predicate noun regardless.

Pronouns

The job of a pronoun is to substitute for a noun. It cannot be used without reference to a nearby noun and it cannot take any modifiers. There are several kinds of pronouns--personal, relative, interrogative. The ones that cause common grammatical errors are the personal ones because they have a variety of forms. These forms provide information about the job being done in the sentence, the gender of the noun in question, and the persons involved in the sentence message.

Forms of Personal Pronouns
First Person (Speaker / Writer)

Singular	Plural
Nominative—I	we
Possessive—my, mine	our, ours

Objective--   me   us

"Nominative" is a case name borrowed from Latin grammar. It indicates a pronoun form working as a subject or a predicate pronoun after a link verb.

Second Person (Spoken To / Written To)

Nominative-- you   you
Possessive-- your, yours   your, yours
Objective--   you   you

Third Person (Spoken/Written About)

(Masculine / Feminine / Neuter)	(No gender distinction in plural)
Nominative-he/ she/ it	they
Possessive-his/ her, hers/ its	their, theirs
Objective—him/her/it	them

Pronouns that can substitute for nouns as subject or predicate noun, either singular or plural--I, you, he, she, it, we, they

as the speaker or speakers--I bought a new car.
                                              We bought a new car.
as the person or persons spoken to--You owe fifty dollars.
as the person or thing spoken about --
                                                  He sells real estate.
                                                  She sells real estate.
                                                  It is very expensive.
                                                  They sell real estate.

Gender in English is natural--male or female for persons and neuter for things and animals.

Other Uses for Pronouns

A few pronouns with slightly different forms are used to show ownership—
             my, mine, your, yours, his, hers, its, our, ours, their, theirs
Some of these precede nouns the way adjectives do—
             my, your, his, her, its, our, their

             I lost my car keys.
             You should save your money.
             He passed his exam.
             She locked her door.

The cat hurt its paw.
We sold our boat.
They are proud of their garden

Some pronouns are used as predicate pronouns after a linking verb--

The red scarf is mine,
The blue one is yours.
Tim said the book was his.
Mary said the briefcase was hers.
The house on the hill is ours.
The workmen admitted the fault was theirs.

Apostrophes are used in pronouns for one special reason--a letter or two has been omitted from the verb or auxiliary that follows--

I am going home/ I'm going home.
You are a good friend/ You're a good friend.
He is a well known artist/ He's a well known artist.
She will be famous some day / She'll be famous some day.
It has been a long day/ It's been a long day.
We are all learning to ski/ We're all learning to ski.
They have been friends for years / They've been friends for years.

Verbs

The principal parts of the verb in English consist of the infinitive (which is the present tense form) -"to play," the present participle--"playing," the simple past tense--"played," and the past participle--"played." The present participle will always consist of the basic form + "ing." The simple past tense and the past participle of regular verbs will always consist of the basic form + "ed."

However, there are many irregular verbs whose past tense and past participle involve internal vowel changes. Despite the growing misuse of some of these irregular forms in popular speech, it is important to master them for the purpose of good writing.

The most common error of this kind is the misuse of the verb pair "lie" and "lay."

They are not interchangeable. "Lie" means "recline" and "lay" means "put."

present tense	present participle	past tense	past participle
lie	lying	lay	(has/have/had) lain
lay	laying	laid	(has/have/had) laid

Obviously, part of the problem is that the past tense of "lie" resembles the present tense of "lay."

Today I lie (recline) in my hammock. Now I am lying in my hammock. Last night I lay in my bed. I have lain in the same bed every night since my childhood.

Today a workman will lay (put) tile in the bathroom. He has been laying tile for many years. Last week he laid tile in a new hotel. He has laid tile in many hotels during his working years.

Notice that the verb "lay" (put) takes an object (N-3), just as the verb "put" does. It can never be used without an object. On the other hand, the verb "lie" never takes an object, just as the verb "recline" does not.

Tenses

There are three simple tenses--Past, Present, and Future--and three compound tenses--Past Perfect, Present Perfect, and Future Perfect. (The term "Perfect" here means "past.")

> Past--The children played.
> Present--Children play.
> Future--Children will play. Children'll play. (The old future form--"shall play" is dead.)

The compound tenses are used in sentences which speak of two time zones.

Past Perfect--the auxiliary "had" + the past participle puts a first action into the more remote past than a second past action.

> The children had played tag before they went into the school building.--two past actions, but one preceded the other.

Present Perfect--the auxiliary "has/have" + the past participle puts one action into the past and continues it into the present.

> The children have played tag since their kindergarten years.

Future Perfect--the auxiliary "will" or its contraction "'ll" + the auxiliary "have" + the past participle. This states an action that will be completed before a specific time in the future.

> Mary will have earned all her tuition money by the time she arrives at college.

The use of the three compound tenses in English is growing less and less common because they necessitate a distinction in time of action for two events in the same sentence. People are less inclined to think the sequence through. Instead, they ignore the perfect tenses and find other constructions or they simply do not make time distinctions. The Future Perfect Tense, in particular, has all but disappeared.

In addition to these common everyday tenses, English has two less important tenses--Progressive and Emphatic.

The progressive tense is formed with the use of "be" as an auxiliary plus an "ing" suffix on the basic form of the main verb. It is used to indicate continued action--

PRESENT	PRESENT PROGRESSIVE
I plan We plan	I am planning We are planning
You plan	You are planning
He/She plans They plan	He/She is planning They are planning

PAST	PAST PROGRESSIVE
I planned We planned	I was planning We were planning
You planned	You were planning
He/She planned They planned	He/She was planning They were planning

FUTURE	FUTURE PROGRESSIVE
I will plan We will plan	I will be planning We will be planning
You will plan	You will be planning
He/She will plan They will plan	He/She will be planning They will be planning

The emphatic tense is formed with the auxiliary "do."

PRESENT	PRESENT EMPHATIC
I like pies We like pies	I do like pies We do like pies
You like pies	You do like pies
He/She likes pies They like pies	He/She does like pies They do like pies.

PAST	PAST EMPHATIC
I liked pies We liked pies	I did like pies We did like pies
You liked pies	You did like pies
He/She liked pies They liked pies	He/She did like pies They did like pies.

FUTURE	FUTURE EMPHATIC
I will like pies We will like pies	No future emphatic forms
You will like pies	
He/She will like pies They will like pies	

Indicative, Imperative, Subjunctive Moods

In addition to indicating time (by means of tenses), action or mere connection (transitive or intransitive), and person (speaker, person spoken to or person spoken about in singular or plural), verbs do one thing more. They have what we might call "coloring"--what traditional grammar calls "mood." This is a way of letting us know whether the verb is being used in a statement of fact or in a command or in a statement that implies a wish, a doubt, or an impossibility.

Most of our everyday sentences provide information of one kind or another. The verbs are said to be in the Indicative mood.

> Our home team won the baseball game.
> I am hungry.
> The cost of living is rising.

These are the basic (indicative mood) forms of sentences that we will be working with.

Another common kind of sentence is an order, command, or suggestion. These verbs are said to be in the Imperative mood.

> Shut the door.
> Watch your step.
> Please listen to me.

The subject in these sentences is said to be understood as "you." The presence or absence of "please" in not significant. We will not be working with imperative sentences because they represent a more advanced form of sentence development.

The third kind of coloring or mood--the Subjunctive-- is the one that causes difficulties in the grammar of some foreign languages. It presents very few problems in English. Our language has been moving away from the subjunctive except for a few common forms. English is more apt to indicate doubt, uncertainty, defiance of fact and even wishfulness by adding other words such as adverbs.

The only common survivors of sentences in the subjunctive mood are a few with "were"--

> If I were you, I would learn to drive.
> I wish I were as rich as some of our politicians.

Verb Functions

1. A verb can make a simple statement in a declarative sentence--
> I like chocolate.
2. A verb can make an emphatic statement with the help of "do"--
> I do like chocolate.
3. A verb can make an emotional statement, usually with the help of an interjection. The use of an exclamation point instead of a period at the end of the sentence intensifies the emotion--
> Damn! I told them I couldn't afford to pay now!

4. A verb can give a command in an imperative sentence. This is a sentence with "you" understood as the subject--
> Answer the phone.

5. A verb can ask a question in an interrogative sentence with the addition of a helper unless the verb is "be" (which does not need any help). The subject and verb are always reversed--
> Are you ready to leave?
> Does this train stop at all stations?
> Can the children watch TV?

6. A verb can express continuing action with the help of "be" plus an –ing ending on the verb--
> My class is going to the museum.
> Strange things have been happening.

CHAPTER 2

Pre-noun Servants--determiners, adjectives, noun adjuncts
Helping Verbs--"be, do, have"
Adverbs
Members of the WH- Club
Free-lance words

Pre-noun servants

Proper nouns can often stand alone in a sentence, but common nouns must be preceded by an informational word called a Determiner. This is a catch-all term standing for a variety of pre-noun servants--article, demonstrative, possessive, quantifier, negator.

Often there will be two or three determiners in front of a common noun. In addition, a noun is frequently preceded by one or two adjectives and/or a noun adjunct.
> The little girl found a penny.
> article+adj+noun+v+article+noun
> Two kind young men helped a blind old woman cross the busy street.
> quantifier+adj+adj+noun+v+article+
> adj+adj+noun+v+article+adj+noun
> I cleaned the parrot cage.
> pron+v+article+noun adjunct+noun

(The adjective form "parrot's" instead of the noun adjunct would be the choice of a conservative writer.)

A pronoun, which is a noun substitute, does not need a determiner.
> We went to a concert.

I took the broken eyeglasses to an optometrist and he replaced them.

Common Irregular Adjectives

Positive	Comparative	Superlative
bad	worse	worst
far	farther, further	farthest, furthest
good	better	best
little	less	least
many, much	more	most
old	older, elder	oldest, eldest

Double comparisons are unacceptable. Either we use the "er/est" method or the "more/ most" method. We cannot use both at the same time.

      Incorrect--most luckiest

      Correct--luckiest

      Correct--most lucky

Helping Verbs (auxiliaries)—Be, Do, Have

These verbs can either be helpers or they can act as a main verb.

Principal Parts

1. be-Infinitive "to be"
   Present Participle "being"
   Past Tense "was/were"
   Past Participle "been"
2. do-Infinitive "to do"
   Present Participle "doing"
   Past Tense "did"
   Past Participle "done"
3. have-Infinitive "to have"
   Present Participle "having"
   Past Tense "had"
   Past Participle "had"

They are needed as helpers to form the perfect tenses and to form the progressive and emphatic forms of verbs. "Do" can also work as a helper to make a sentence negative or emphatic. "Be" is needed to help form the passive voice.

Conjugation of "Be"
Present Tense

Singular	Plural
I am/ I'm	we are/ we're
you are/ you're	same as singular

he (she, it) is/ he's (she's,it's)   they are/ they're

Past Tense

I was	we were
you were	same as singular
he (she, it) was	they were

Future Tense

I will be/ I'll be	we will be/ we'll be
you will be/ you'll be	same as singular
he (she, it) will be/ he'll (she'll,it'll) be	they will be/ they'll be

Present Perfect Tense

I have been / I've been	we have been/ we've been
you have been / you've been	same as singular
he (she, it) has been/ he's (she's, it's) been	they have been/ they've been

"Have" is often shortened to apostrophe plus "ve" and "has" is shortened to apostrophe plus "s."

Past Perfect Tense

I had been/ I'd been	we had been/ we'd been
you had been/ you'd been	same as singular
he (she,it) had been/ he'd (she'd, it'd) been	they had been/they'd been

"Had" is often shortened to apostrophe + "d."

Future Perfect Tense

I will have been/ I'll have been	we will have been/ we'll have been
you will have been/ you'll have been	same as singular
he (she, it) will have been/ he'll (she'll, it'll) have been	they will have been/ they'll have been

All the shortened forms are used only in spoken English and informal writing.

Conjugation of "Do"
Present Tense

Singular	Plural
I do	we do
you do	same as singular
he(she, it) does	they do

Past Tense

I did	we did
you did	same as singular
he (she,it) did	they did

Future Tense

I will do/ I'll do	we will do/ we'll do
you will do/ you'll do	same as singular
he (she, it) will do/ he'll (she'll, it'll) do	they will do/they'll do

Present Perfect Tense

I have done/ I've done

you have done/ you've done

he (she, it) has done/ he's (she's, it's) done

we have done/ we've done

same as singular

they have done/ they've done

Past Perfect Tense

I had done/ I'd done

you had done/ you'd done

he (she,it) had done/ he'd (she'd, it'd) done

we had done/ we'd done

same as singular

they had done/ they'd done

Future Perfect Tense

I will have done/ I'll have done

you will have done/you'll have done

he (she,it) will have done

he'll (she'll,it'll) have done

we will have done/we'll have done

same as singular

they will have done

they'll have done

Reminder—"Shall," formerly used like "will" as a helper, is now obsolete.

Conjugation of "Have"

Present Tense

Singular

I have

you have

he (she, it) has

Plural

we have

same as singular

they have

Past Tense

I had

you had

he (she, it) had

we had

same as singular

they had

Future Tense

I will have/ I'll have

you will have/ you'll have

he(she, it) will have

he'll (she'll, it'll) have

we will have/we'll have

same as singular

they will have

they'll have

Present Perfect Tense

I have had/ I've had

you have had/ you've had

he (she, it) has had

he's (she's, it's) had

we have had/ we've had

same as singular

they have had/ they've had

Past Perfect Tense

I had had/ I'd had

you had had / you'd had

he (she, it) had had

he'd (she'd, it'd) had

we had had /we'd had

same as singular

they had had / they'd had

Future Perfect Tense

I will have had / I'll have had

we will have had/ we'll

	have had
you will have had / you'll have had	same as singular
he (she, it) will have had	they will have had
he (she'll, it'll) have had	they'll have had

Comparison of Adverbs

Descriptive adverbs also have three forms--positive, comparative, and superlative. They usually make use of the "more/most" method--

slowly, more slowly, most slowly.

However, adverbs that do not end in "ly" are compared by the "er/est" used for comparison of adjectives--

soon, sooner, soonest

Common Irregular Adverbs

Positive	Comparative	Superlative
badly	worse	worst
little	less	least
much	more	most

Many non-descriptive adverbs cannot be compared- "here, there, now, then, when, why, where, how."

APPENDIX B

PUNCTUATION

Punctuation is the system of traffic signals that regulates the flow of the reader's attention. A comma means " brief pause." A semicolon means " longer pause." A colon means "stop and look ahead." A period means "full stop."

The comma is the signal that has the most varied uses, and for this reason, it is the one that causes writers the most trouble. Generally speaking, if you are in doubt about whether or not to put a comma in a certain part of the sentence, leave it out. Putting a comma where it doesn't belong betrays your ignorance. Leaving it out may just look like oversight. Fewer commas are used these days because of the overall tendency in America to speed things up. However, there still remain places in the sentence where commas are required.

If we think about a sentence as a standard construction, we can say it has a beginning, a middle, and an end. In a normal everyday sentence, every one of the basic patterns listed in Chapter 1 begins with the subject, N-1. Next comes the middle-- the verb, with or without auxiliaries and modifiers. The pattern may end there, or the pattern may go on to include a complement such as N-2, N-3, Nn-1, Nn-3, predicate adjective, or predicate adverb.

It is taken for granted that we put a period at the end of every sentence that makes a statement and a question mark at the end of every question. There is no occasion in serious writing when we would use two question marks together. Also, English does not put a question mark at the beginning. An exclamation mark instead of a period at the end is a rare necessity. It is better avoided. A dash at the end is incorrect.

The Comma

At the beginning of a sentence--
A comma at the beginning of a sentence before the subject word occurs tells the reader to pause and pay attention because the message is about to begin.

152

The preliminary words that may precede the subject are easy to recognize.
1. throat-clearers—
> Well, it's hard to answer that.
> Mm, I think so too.
> So, let's make a deal.
> Oh, it's about four o'clock.

2. attention-getters--
> Mr. Chairman, I call for a vote.
> Mom, Billy took my notebook.
> Hey, that's my parking space.

3. introducers--
> He shouted, "I saw you hit that homer."
> The saying is, "Haste makes waste."
> The problem is, we don't have enough money.

4. responses--
> Yes, I'll drive.
> No, the necklace is not for sale.
> All right, I give up.

5. windups--these are groups of words that are like the motions of a pitcher getting ready to throw the ball. These word groups always contain a verb form.
> a) They are often verbal adjectives or verbal adjective phrases--
>> Amazed at the high cost, Mr. Brown canceled his order.
>> Cheering loudly, the spectators encouraged the team.
>> Broken into little pieces, the plate lay on the floor.
>> Surprised, the driver jammed on the brakes.
> b) They can be infinitives or infinitive phrases. These are often editorial comment, revealing the attitude of the writer—
>> To tell the truth, we don't want to see him.
>> To sum up, the profits are satisfactory.

6. describers--These are often prepositional phrases that give information about the time or place or sequence of the action to be stated in the main part of the sentence. Generally, if the phrase consists of more than three words, we use a comma. If the description consists of one or two words, we do not use a comma.
> At noon a whistle blew.
> After a long wait, the patient was admitted to the hospital.
> With a shake of her head, the nurse closed the door.

7. transitional words--these are words used in a series of sentences to ease the flow of ideas--
> However, the committee…
> Moreover,…………
> Consequently,………
> In conclusion,...

8. dependent clauses as preliminary statements-- In most cases these could be put at the end of the sentence instead, if the writer prefers. If the dependent clause is placed after the main clause, it is set off by a comma only occasionally. See below.

> Because the hurricane hit our beach, our house was flooded.
> Our house was flooded because the hurricane hit our beach.
> After Mrs. Brown got her driver's license, she became very independent.
> Mrs. Brown became very independent after she got her driver's license.

As a general rule, if the sentence begins with any kind of verb or verb form, put a comma after it.

In the middle of a sentence--
1. interrupters--

> You should, I think, learn to use a dictionary.
> People, generally speaking, like to watch sports.
> Lions, for example, cannot be really tamed.

2. explainers--

> a) echoes (appositives): These are second nouns that give additional information about the noun to their left.
>> Mr. Black, a private detective, carries a gun.
>> The child was fond of Donald Duck, a Disney character.
> b) identifiers: These are clauses (sentence patterns with relative or subordinating introducers) that are not necessary for the identification of the noun they follow.
>> That red house, where I was born, dates back to 1830.

When there is a clause that is necessary for the identification of the noun, no commas are used. The subject is too general.

> The house where I was born dates back to 1830.
> Unnecessary—The fugitive, who jumped the fence, was finally caught.

The subject "fugitive" is specific. Therefore we set off the following clause with commas.

> Necessary--The man who jumped the fence was finally caught.

The subject "man" is too general. We need the following clause for identification. Therefore we do not use commas.

> Unnecessary—The Volvo, which is described on page one, is a bargain.
> Necessary--The car that is described on page one is a bargain.

Occasionally, when the interrupter is almost totally divorced from the sentence message, dashes are used instead of commas--

> The movie--and I must say it was awful--started a half hour late.

Dashes are to be used with care, since they give the sentence a tone of breezy informality that is not always appropriate.

Parentheses, on the other hand, make the sentence seem serious, even scholarly.

> That building (erected in 1914) was our city's first skyscraper.

At the end of the sentence--after the message (the sentence pattern)

1. tag questions: These are not really questions. They are used in conversation to soften the expression of your opinion--

> I love sunsets, don't you.
> He certainly can hit a ball, can't he?
> That's a beautiful picture, isn't it?
> We'll have a good time, won't we?

2. trailers: These are subordinate clauses that seem to be an afterthought. They are usually introduced by "unless," "although," and "though."

> I'm going to go to Europe, though I can't afford it.
> Spinach is healthful, although many people don't like it.
> We'll take the train, unless you have a better idea.

3. quotation closers:

> "I'm going to the movies," she said.

(Notice that the comma goes inside the quotation mark.)

Other Punctuation Marks

1. semicolon: A semicolon represents a longer pause than a comma does.

> a) a semicolon is used to connect two equally important sentence patterns when we choose not to use the conjunctions "and, but, or, nor." It is the instant between our attention to the first statement and our attention to the next statement.
>
> > Greenland is icy; Iceland is volcanic.
>
> b) a semicolon is used to separate items in a series when commas are used within the series.
>
> > The speakers were a journalist, in English; a professor, in French, and a lawyer, in German.

Normally a series--"journalist," professor," and "lawyer"--would be set off by commas, but since the prepositional phrase after each noun must be set off by commas, we use the stronger punctuation device-- the semicolon. Unfortunately, we cannot be consistent and use a semicolon after "French," because of the "and." It works as powerfully as a semicolon when used with a comma.

Contrary to usage with a comma, a semicolon is always placed outside the quotation mark. (The period goes inside.)

> Edith recited "Ode on a Grecian Urn"; John recited "The Charge of the Light Brigade."

2. colon: The colon tells the reader to look ahead.

a) it joins two equally important sentence patterns when the first one is a generalization and the second one is an example.

> The man was hard to get along with: he had a quick temper.

b) it introduces a formal list.

> The guest's requirements are as follows: bottled water, hot tea, today's newspaper, and fresh flowers.

(It is incorrect to omit the words "as follows" before the colon.

c) it follows the salutation in a business letter

> Dear Mr. Morgan:

3. single and double dash:

a) The single dash can follow a series in order to emphasize a summary which is signaled by a word like "these," "those," "all."

> Red, yellow, blue—these are the primary colors.

> Oranges, lemons, limes, grapefruit—all are citrus fruits.

b) a pair of dashes can set off an interrupting expression in a sentence when the interruption is more dramatic than one requiring commas.

> The scenery on the stage—it must have cost a fortune—was beautiful.

> Less dramatic--The scenery on the stage, while quite unusual, was beautiful.

Caution--do not end a sentence with a dash unless you are writing a dialogue in which the speaker stops abruptly.

> The prisoner answered, "I was a stranger in the village and I couldn't believe--" He threw up his hands and said no more.

4. parentheses: A pair of parentheses is often used to set off sentence interrupters when the information being given is an extra, something not really necessary.

> William Shakespeare (1564-1616) was an actor as well as playwright.

5. quotation marks, single and double: Double quotation marks are used far more frequently than single quotation marks.

Double--

    a) for a direct quotation-- to enclose the exact words of a speaker

        The fisherman said, "No fish biting today."

(Note the positions of comma and period and the use of a capital letter on the first word of the quotation.)

An indirect quotation does not use quotation marks.

        The fisherman said that no fish were biting that day.

    b) double quotation marks are used to enclose the exact words said or written by someone else and used in one's own writing.

        The defendant called his accuser "a nasty little pipsqueak."

        The words "all men are created equal" are familiar to anyone who has studied the Declaration of Independence.

(When we use quotations in this way, we are obliged to state where the words came from.)

    c) since the title of a book or magazine is underlined in writing (to instruct the printer to put it in italics), a shorter unit of the book or magazine--the title of a chapter or article--is put into double quotation marks.

        The third chapter, "Facing Winter Hardship," in *A History of the First Colonies* is the most interesting.

        Happenings on Broadway" is the title of Wilson's column in *Weekly Theater News.*

    d) double quotation marks enclose titles of songs and plays .

        The tenor sang Schubert's "Ave Maria."

        Have you ever seen O'Neill's "Desire Under the Elms"?

Single quotation marks are used for a quotation inside another quotation--

        "You must believe me," said the lawyer. "I definitely heard the defendant shouting 'Give me a second chance.'"

APPENDIX C

ANSWERS TO EXERCISES

CHAPTER 1

Exercise 1
1. my--speaker
   their--Nelsons
   she--mother
2. her--queen
   she--queen
   it--crown
   her-queen
3. its--fire
   their--firefighters
   it--fire
4. his--fisherman
   their-spectators
5. it--dog
   them--ushers

Exercise 2
1. N-1   N-3
   architect   library
2. N-1   N-2   N-3
   engineers bridge inspection
3. N-1
   fame
4. N-1   N-3
   children   games
5. N-1   N-2   N-3
   mayor champion trophy
6. N-1   N-3
   show spectators
7. N-1   N-3   Nn-3
   law   citizens   senators
8. N-1   N-3   Nn-3
   committee Mr. Perkins chairman

9. N-1
   father

10. N-1   N-2   N-3
    cat   mother   mouse

Exercise 3
1. (An) N-1   actionVintr   (on-the-moon)
   astronaut   walked
2. (The) (old) N-1   actionVtr (a) N-3
                Violinist played   solo
3. (Our) (new) N-1   Vlink   pred. adj
               business   was   successful
4. (A) (beautiful) N-1   actionVtr (the) (young) N-3   Nn-3adj
                 voice   made   singer famous
5. (A) (low-sodium) N-1   Vlink (a) (sensible) Nn-1
                  diet   is   choice
6. (The) N-1   actionVtr (the) (new) N-3   Nn-3
         children called   puppy Brownie
7. (A) N-1   actionV tr (my) N-2 (a) (cheap) N-3
       dealer sold   brother   car
8. (Some) N-1   actionVintr (very slowly)
          people   walk
9. (My) N-1   Vlink (a) (certified) Nn-1
       professor   was   expert
10. (The) (band) N-1   Vlink (right)   PredAdv/place
                 leader   is   here

Exercise 4
1. (In- the-trash) I found (an) (old) (photograph) album
             N-1   action Vtr   N-3

2. (A) (long) trail (through-an-evergreen-forest-near-the-coast- of-
            N-1--fragment (no verb)
   northern-Oregon)
3. (An) attendant (finally) scrubbed (the) floor clean
            N-1   action Vtr   N-3 Nn-3adj
4. (My) (best friend's) father was (the) speaker (at-our
                    N-1   Vlink   Nn-1
   commencement)
5. (The) music (of-a-brass-band) (always) gives (the) crowd pleasure
         N-1   actionVtr N-2   N-3
6. (The) (football) team played (enthusiastically) (in-spite-of-the-rain)
              N-1   action Vintr
7. (The) (senior) class (unanimously) made   Ed (their) spokesman
              N-1   actionVtr N-3   Nn-3

8. Everyone (hoping for-sunny-weather on-our-vacation-trip)
  N-1--fragment (no verb)
9. Mrs. Smith was unrecognizable (in-the-dim-light-of-the-garage)
   N-1   Vlink pred adj
10. (The) (usual) time (for-our-meeting) was noon
     N-1   Vlink Nn-1

CHAPTER 2

Exercise 5
1. Noun--tree
 A--article
 large--adjective
 Noun--roof
 our--possessive pronoun
 Noun--storm
 the--article
 violent--adjective
2. Noun--damage
 The--article
  storm--noun adjunct
3. Noun--umbrella
  my--possessive pronoun
4. Noun--volunteers
 No--negator
 Noun--fire
 the--article
 sudden--adjective
5. Noun--answer
 Dorothy's--possessive noun
 Noun--question
 our--possessive pronoun
 simple--adjective
6. Noun--leader
 The--article
  band--noun adjunct
 Noun--jacket
  a--article
  stylish--adjective
  red--adjective
7. Noun--tires
  the--article
  new--adjective
 Noun--car
  our--possessive pronoun
  old--adjective

8. Noun--dog
   That--demonstrative
   muddy--adjective
   Noun--bath
   a--article
   good--adjective
9. Noun--children
   Our--possessive pronoun
   Noun--reason
   the--article
   Noun--cancellation
   the--article
   Noun--party
   their--possessive pronoun
10. Noun--spectators
    many--quantifier
    Noun--flags
    little--adjective
    Noun--athletes
    their--possessive pronoun
    favorite—adjective

Exercise 6
1. has--auxiliary
2. do--aux
3. should--modal
4. could--modal
   have--aux
5. will--modal
   have--aux
6. may--modal
   have--aux
   been--aux
7. is--aux
8. ought to--modal
9. do---aux (n't --drop this negator)
   might--modal
   have--aux
10. ---

Exercise 7
1. up
   destroyed
2. down
   destroyed
3. ---

(down--preposition)

4. ---
   (up--preposition)
5. out
   discarded

6. (outside, inside---adverbs)
7. ---
   (through--preposition)
8. through
   skimmed
9. over
   examine
10. up
    search for

Exercise 8
1. often--frequency
   rather--degree
   carefully--manner
2. here--place
   continually--frequency
3. however--transition
   totally--degree
   carefully--manner
4. unfortunately--editorial comment
   not--negator
   thoroughly--degree
5. nearly--degree
   indignantly--manner
   immediately--time

CHAPTER 3

Exercise 9
1. at the palace--adjectival, mod. "watchers"
   of the spy's approach--adverbial, mod."warned"
   by a messenger from the sentries outside the city wall--adverbial,
    mod. "warned"
   from the sentries outside the city wall--adjectival, mod.
    "messenger"
   outside the city wall--adjectival, mod."sentries"
2. In the living room--adverbial, mod. "read"
    from the works of Shakespeare--adverbial, mod. "read"
    of Shakespeare--adjectival, mod. "works"

in the kitchen--adverbial, mod."dozed"
with a cup of tea on the table in front of him--adverbial,
mod."dozed"
of tea--adjectival, mod. "cup"
on the table in front of him--adjectival, mod. "tea"
in front of him--adjectival, mod. "table"
of him--adjectival, mod. "front"

3. without tickets--adjectival, mod. "arrivals"
on a long line beside the curb--adverbial, mod."waited"
beside the curb--adjectival, mod "line"
with tickets--adjectival, mod. "people"
to the inner lobby of the theater--adverbial, mod. "admitted"
of the theater--adjectival, mod. "lobby"

4. Before her vacation trip--adverbial, mod. "been"
about its cost--adverbial, mod. "anxious"
during her travels--adverbial, mod."put"
out of her mind--adverbial, mod. "put"

5. Between the two houses--adverbial, mod. "strolled"
with a bandage on its left paw--adjectival, mod. "cat"
on its left paw--adjectival, mod. "paw"

Exercise 10
1. repairing-clocks--Nn-1
2. Swimming-laps-in-a-pool--N-1
3. trying-foreign-recipes--N-3
4. buying-new-gadgets--Nn-1
5. Waiting-for-the-bus-on-a-cold-night--N-1
6. my-winning-the-contest---object of preposition "at"
7. feeding-the-animals--N-3
8. not-skipping-any-classes--Nn-1
9. revealing-the-donor's-name--object of preposition "to"
10. Not-eating-vegetables--N-1

Exercise 11
1. verbal noun ("repairing") + N-3 (its object "clocks")
2. verbal noun ("swimming") + N-3 (its object "laps") + prepositional
   phrase modifier ("in-a-pool")
3. verbal noun ("trying")+ noun cluster as N-3 ("foreign recipes")
4. verbal noun ("buying") + noun cluster as N-3 ("new gadgets")
5. verbal noun ("waiting") + prepositional phrase as modifier ("for-
   the-bus") + second prepositional phrase as modifier ("on-a-cold-
   night")
6. possessive pronoun ("my") + verbal noun ("winning") + noun
   cluster as N-3 ("the contest")
7. verbal noun ("feeding") noun cluster as N-3 ("the animals")

8. negator ("not")+ verbal noun ("skipping") + noun cluster as N-3 ("any classes")
9. verbal noun (" revealing") + noun cluster as N-3 ("the donor's name")
10. negator (" not") + verbal noun (" eating") + noun as N-3 ("vegetables")

Exercise 12
1. Following-the-wrong-trail, dangling--does not modify "hours."
   Correction--Following-the-wrong-trail, the hikers lost hours.
2. Watching-the-greyhound-races, I forgot my dental appointment.
   Correct sentence
3. Crowded-into-a-corner-by-autograph-hunters, dangling--does not modify "sympathies" Correction--My sympathies were with the famous singer crowded-into-a-corner-by-autograph-hunters.
4. Having-swept-through-the-village, dangling--does not modify "damage" Correction--Having-swept-through-the-village, the storm did much damage.
5. Having-introduced-the-speaker--dangling--does not modify "everyone." It is not possible to move "chairman' closer to the verbal phrase without having an awkward sentence. In cases like this. we expand the phrase into a subordinate clause--Everyone saw the chairman leave the room after he had introduced the speaker.
6. Traced-in-ink, dangling--does not modify "leader." Correction--Our leader found the map, traced-in-ink, easy to read. This version, while grammatically correct, is still awkward because the two verbs are referring to differences in time. Again, the sentence would be improved by expanding the verbal phrase into a relative clause--Our leader found the map, which had been traced in ink, easy to read.
7. seated-on-a-soapbox, dangling--does not modify "crowd." Correction--Seated-on-a-soapbox, the clown waved to the crowd.
8. Broken-beyond-repair, dangling--does not modify "salesman." Correction--The salesman regretted the loss of the vase, broken beyond repair.
9. Brought-down-by-a-single-shot, dangling--does not modify "I." Correction--I picked up the bird, brought-down-by-a-single-shot.
10. Having-been-delayed-on-the-road, dangling--does not modify "ferryboat." Once again, simply moving the verbal phrase would not produce a usable sentence. We need to expand the phrase into a clause, a subordinate one--"The ferryboat sailed without us because we had been delayed on the road." It is usually always a time difference in the verbs that makes this expansion necessary.

Exercise 13
Reminder--Dropping adjective phrases can eliminate interesting
 details, but does not affect any necessary sentence pattern elements.
 Verbal noun phrases cannot be dropped.
1. Pitching-a-no-hit-game-in-baseball--noun phrase as N-1. Cannot be
 dropped.
2. facing-Broadway--adjective phrase modifying "bank," can be
 dropped--The bank closed last week.
3. digging-in-a-nearby-field--adjective phrase modifying "man," can be
 dropped--We watched a man.
4. gathering-wood-for-a-fire--noun phrase as N-3. Cannot be dropped.
5. Seeing-the-danger-instantly--adjective phrase modifying "ranger,"
 can be dropped--The ranger pulled me to one side.
6. ransacking-the-desk-drawers--noun phrase as object of the
 preposition "after." Cannot be dropped.
7. My-missing-the-train--noun phrase as N-1. Cannot be dropped.
8. Wondering-about-the-former-owner-of-the-house--adjective clause
 modifying "we," can be dropped--We explored the attic.
9. blowing-in-the-wind--adjective phrase modifying "flags," can be
 dropped--From our balcony we saw the flags.
10. Becoming-a-fine-pianist--noun phrase as N-1. Cannot be dropped.

Exercise 14
1. (to-win-the-mayoral election) Nn-1
2. (To-learn-Latin) N-1
3. (to-visit-the-palace) adverb modifying adjective "anxious"
4. (to-teach-the-value-of-patience) Nn-1
5. (to-trap-the-criminal) adjective modifying "plan"
6. (to-take-a-long-vacation) N-3
7. (To-Advance-Knowledge) Nn-1
8. (not-to-tease-the-dog) N-3
9. (To-have-my-own-credit-card) N-1
0. (to-build-a-rocket) N-3

Exercise 15
1. to win-infinitive, the mayoral election-noun cluster as N-3
2.To learn- infinitive, Latin-N-3
3. to visit--infinitive, the palace-noun cluster as N-3
4. to teach-infinitive, the value of patience-noun cluster as N-3
5. to trap-infinitive, the criminal-noun cluster as N-3
6. to take-infinitive, a long vacation-noun cluster as N-3
7. to advance-infinitive, knowledge-noun as N-3
8. not-negator, to tease-infinitive, the dog-noun cluster as N-3
9. to have-infinitive, my own credit card-noun cluster as N-3
10. to build-infinitive, a rocket-noun cluster as N-3

Exercise 16

1. Displaying-his-splendid-tail--adjective phrase modifying "peacock"
   for-me-to-feed-him--adverb modifying "waited" (This is an infinitive
   phrase at its maximum. It is actually a telescoped clause consisting
   of "me" as the subject of the verbal "feed" and "for" as a preposition
   of which the whole infinitive phrase as the object.)
2. to-catch-an-early-train--infinitive phrase as N-3 of verb "hoped"
   waiting-for-the-taxi-noun phrase as N-1 of verb "kept"
   getting-to-the-station-on-time--noun phrase as object of preposition
   "from"
3. the-tailor-to-shorten-her-coat--infinitive phrase as N-3 of "asked"
   (This is another infinitive with its own N-1 "tailor.")
   to-look-dowdy--infinitive phrase as N-3 of verb "want"
4. Crabgrass-growing-vigorously--noun phrase as N-1 of verb "was
   taking over"
5. Hanging-pictures-in-a-new-apartment--noun phrase as N-1 of verb
   "proved"
   to-be-a-test-of-my-patience--N-3 of "proved"
6. doing-the-crossword-puzzle--noun phrase as object of preposition
   "about"
7. to-be-evacuated-by-the-rescue-crew--infinitive phrase as N-3 of verb
   "refused"
8. Flying-a-kite-noun phrase as N-1 of verb "seemed"
9. Having-planned-the-expedition-carefully---adjective phrase
   modifying "Foster"
10. to-interrupt-the-man-telling-a-long-and-tiresome-story--infinitive
    phrase modifying adjective "ready"
    telling-a-long-and-tiresome--story--adjective phrase modifying
    "man"

Exercise 17

1. four or five--pair of quantifiers modifying noun "hikers"
   coffee, doughnuts, and gossip--noun series, object of preposition
   "for"
2. The furnace shut down, a water pipe broke, the dog ran away, and
   the cook went to bed with a headache--series of independent
   clauses forming a supersentence
3. pick wildflowers, be careless with matches, or forget about bears--
   series of verb clusters as predicate of sentence whose N-1 is
   "You"
   in safety and in harmony with nature--pair of adverbial prepositional
   phrases modifying verb "live"
4. satin and lace--pair of noun adjuncts modifying noun "dresses"

neither Gertrude nor Eliza--pair of nouns as N-3 of verb "pleased"
("Neither" is the usual accompaniment of "nor." They then act as a
single coordinate conjunction.)
5. theaters, restaurants, and museums--series of nouns as N-1 of verb
"interested"
interested Don but bored his mother and father--pair of verb
clusters as predicate of sentence
mother and father--pair of nouns as N-3 of verb "bored"

Exercise 18
1. not very truthfully--adverb cluster modifying verb "maintained," head
word "truthfully"
totally honest--adjective cluster as predicate adjective after verb
"was," head word "honest"
2. rather grumpy-- adjective cluster modifying noun "clerk," head word
"grumpy"
barely audible--adjective cluster modifying noun "tones," head word
"audible"
most obviously--adverb cluster modifying verb "lost," head word
"obviously"
3. fresh as a daisy--adjective cluster as predicate adjective after verb
"looked," head word "fresh"
happy as a lark--adjective cluster as predicate adjective after verb
"seemed," head word "happy"
really gaudy--adjective cluster modifying noun "boxes," head word
"gaudy"
4. more slowly than usual--adverb cluster modifying verb "walked,"
head word "slowly"
extremely snowy--adjective cluster modifying noun "playground,"
head word " snowy"
5. too eager--adjective cluster modifying noun "waiter," head word
"eager"
quite dramatically--adverb cluster modifying verb "handed," head
word "dramatically"

Exercise 19
1. an iceberg--head word "iceberg," N-1 for verb " struck"
the cargo ship--head word "ship," N-3 for verb "struck"
2. a Florida beach--head word "beach," N-1 for verb "is"
our favorite winter destination--head word "destination," Nn-1 for
verb "is"
3. The old man living by the lake--head word "man," N-1 for verb
"went"
the lake--head work "lake," object of preposition "by"
his dog--head word "dog," N-1 for verb "was barking"

4. the shop window--head word "window," object of preposition "in"
   one blue bottle--head word "bottle," N-1 for verb "caught"
   the afternoon sunlight--head word "sunlight," N-3 for verb "caught"
5. the stranded party boat--head word "boat," N-1 for verb "drew"
   curious glances--head word "glances," N-3 for verb "drew"
   the passing ferry--head word "ferry," object of the preposition "from"
6. This necklace inherited from my grandmother--head word
   "necklace," N-1 for verb "is"
   my grandmother--head word "grandmother," object of preposition
   "from"
7. A young man with a shaved head--head word "man," N-1 for verb
   "was"
   a shaved head-- head word "head," object of preposition "with"
   the manager of the hair salon--head word "manager," Nn-1 for verb
   "was"
8. Maria's new admirer--head word "admirer," N-1 for verb "sent"
   one dozen long-stemmed roses--head word "roses," N-3 for verb
   "sent"
9. the steamship company--head word "company," N-1 for verb "said"
   the Titanic--head word "Titanic," N-1 for verb "was"
   the safest ship afloat--head word "ship," Nn-1 for verb "was:"
10. The boy with the lollipop in one hand--head word "boy," N-1 for verb
    "wanted"
    the lollipop--head word "lollipop," object of preposition "with"
    one hand--head word "hand," object of preposition "in"
    my frisky little puppy--head word "puppy," N-3 for verb "hold"
    the other--head word pronoun "other," object of preposition "with"

Exercise 20
1. swallowed the bait on my hook--head word " swallowed" + the bait
   on my hook--noun cluster as N-3
2. must have noticed the tulip display--head word "noticed," "must" as
   modal, "have" as auxiliary+ the tulip display--noun cluster as N-3
3. never could remember his teacher's name--
   head word "remember," "never" negative adverb modifying
   "remember," "could "   as auxiliary + noun cluster as N-3
4. has been a tradition for many years--head word "been," "has" as
   auxiliary + noun cluster as Nn-1
5. barked at my visitors--head word "barked" + prepositional phrase
   modifying "barked"
6. crossed the street--head word "crossed" + noun cluster as N-3
   came around the corner--head word--"came" + prepositional phrase
   modifying "came"
7. always tell hikers to beware of the bears--head word "hikers,"
   "always" adverb modifying "tell" + infinitive phrase as N-3

beware of the bears--head word "beware" + prepositional phrase modifying "beware"

8. are a concern of many towns and villages relying upon them for a municipal water supply--head word "are" +noun cluster as N-3

9. did not bring enough rain to the little prairie town that was suffering a drought--head word "bring," "did" as auxiliary, "not" as negator + noun cluster "enough rain" as N-3 + prepositional phrase modifying "bring"

   was suffering a drought--head word "suffering," "was" as auxiliary + noun cluster as N-3

10. have been disappearing from people's gardens in the last few years--head word "disappearing," "have" as auxiliary, "been" as auxiliary + prepositional phrase--"from people's gardens" modifying "disappearing" + prepositional phrase "in the last few years" modifying "disappearing"

Exercise 21

1.The very rich people in the summer cottages--noun cluster, head word "people"

   very rich--adjective cluster, head word "rich"

   the summer cottages--noun cluster, head word "cottages"

   almost always stayed on the beach until dusk--verb cluster, head word "stayed"

   almost always--adverb cluster, head word "always"

   the beach--noun cluster, head word "beach"

2. The rather simple task of building a model igloo --noun cluster, head word "task"

   rather simple--adjective cluster, head word "simple"

   a model igloo--noun cluster, head word "igloo"

   will be completed in a few weeks--verb cluster, head word "completed"

   a few weeks--noun cluster, head word "weeks"

3. Very generously--adverb cluster, head word "generously"

   the owner of the motorboat--noun cluster, head word "owner"

   the motorboat--noun cluster, head word "motorboat"

   lent it to the local Boy Scouts--verb cluster, head word "lent"

   the local Boy Scouts-noun cluster, head word "Boy Scouts"

4. Every daffodil along the garden path--noun cluster, head word "daffodil"

   the garden path--noun cluster, head word "path"

   had disappeared quite mysteriously--verb cluster, head word "disappeared"

   quite mysteriously--adverb cluster, head word "mysteriously"

5. Only really expert divers in wet suits--noun cluster, head word "divers"

   really expert--adjective cluster, head word "expert"

should be looking for treasure in that sunken ship--verb cluster, head word "looking for"
that sunken ship--noun cluster, head word "ship"

CHAPTER 4

Exercise 22
1. swamp (has been) drying out--independent clause
   alligators (have been) showing signs--independent clause
   Because the drought has lasted a long time--subordinate clause
   which depend upon water--relative clause (adjectival) modifies
   "alligators"
2. all lined up--independent clause
   whose baggage had been lost--relative clause (adjectival) modifies
   "tourists"
   while manager shouted--subordinate clause
3. detective questioned everyone--independent clause
   who had no sympathy--relative clause (adjectival) modifies
   "detective"
   although no one had anything--subordinate clause
4. time has come--independent clause
   when you need license--relative clause (adverbial) modifies "come"
5. I wondered (something)--independent clause
   why we get up--buried question ("had to" is the past tense of "must,"
   a droppable modal)
   since bus leave-- subordinate clause
6. reporters wanted to know (something)--independent clause
   who covered races--relative clause--(adjectival) modifies
   "reporters"
   whose canoe turned over--buried question
7. we waited --independent clause
   while mechanic looked at engine--subordinate clause("looked at"=a
   verb + particle meaning "examined.")
8. children asked mother (something)--independent clause
   where she put candy--buried question
   which they collected--relative clause (adjectival) modifies "candy"
9. nobody noticed (something)--independent clause
   that puppy was left--subordinate clause (This is a passive-voice
   clause with a dropped subject--See Chapter 5. The normal active-
   voice version would be "we left puppy." In this case the sentence
   would read "Nobody noticed that we had left the puppy behind."
   This would still be a subordinate clause.)
10. salesman drove Walter--independent clause
    Walter showed interest--independent clause

Exercise 23
1. sentence fragment (subordinate clause)
    If we drop the subordinate conjunction "although," we have an acceptable independent clause--"The students had double-checked their experiments during the chemistry exam."
    Alternatively, we could add an independent clause to the fragment and get a supersentence--"Although the students had double-checked their experiments during the chemistry exam, most of them received a failing grade."
2. acceptable sentence--"the lights went out" is an independent clause to which the relative clause ("when lightning struck the building") is attached.
3. sentence fragment. This whole statement is a subject without a predicate. (N- 1 + nothing)
    Reminder-- A predicate must always contain a verb. It may or may not also contain a complement. (see glossary.)
    "which had set up its tent on the outskirts of the village" is a relative clause acting as an adjective to modify "circus." We need to add a predicate, for example, "delighted the children." Now we have N-1 + Vtrans. + N-3--an independent clause which is an acceptable sentence pattern. "A traveling circus, which had set up its tent on the outskirts of the village, delighted the children."
4. This is a sentence fragment like that in #3--a subject without a predicate. (N-1 + nothing). "where the elephant had dislodged some rocks," a relative clause modifying the noun "part," is like a droppable adjective. Again we need to add a predicate--"tested our endurance." Now we have N-1 + Vtrans.+ N-3, making an acceptable sentence pattern. "The most dangerous part of the trail, where the elephant had dislodged some rocks, tested our endurance."
5. acceptable sentence consisting of an independent clause "The students talked among themselves" plus a relative clause "while the lecturer picked up his notes" modifying "talked" and a relative clause "which he had dropped on the floor" modifying "notes."
6. acceptable sentence--an independent clause "the band of tourists entered the shops that lined the esplanade." This independent clause contains a relative clause ("that lined the esplanade") which modifies "shops." The preceding clause ("Because the tour guide was lingering over his beer at the little cafe on the corner") is subordinate.
    As long as there is an independent clause to provide the foundation, technically any number of subordinate and relative clauses can be attached. The result, however, can be an overloaded sentence that slows down the reader.
7. sentence fragment—a subject without a predicate (N-1 + nothing)."who was very particular about the temperature of the

auditorium" is a relative clause modifying "singer." We need to supply a predicate, such as "refused to perform" (Vtrans + N-3). The N-3 is an infinitive acting as a noun. "The singer, who was very particular about the temperature of the auditorium, refused to perform."

8. acceptable sentence--"wagons headed for the frontier" (N-1 + Vtrans +N-3)

   ("headed for" is a verb with a meaning-changing particle that goes along with it.)

9. sentence fragment--another subject without a predicate (N-1 + nothing).

   The relative clause("who were usually skeptical of foreign headliners") modifying "critics" does not supply the necessary missing predicate. We need to add at least an intransitive verb or a transitive verb with an object. "Broadway's theater critics who were usually skeptical of foreign headliners applauded" (N-1 + Vintrans) or "Broadway's theater critics who were usually skeptical of foreign headliners applauded the French star" (N-1 + Vtrans + N-3)

10. sentence fragment--this is one long subordinate clause that cannot stand alone. We can drop the introductory subordinate conjunction "since" and end up with an acceptable sentence--"we all needed a good night's sleep after our strenuous afternoon running in the senior citizens' marathon" (N-1 + Vtrans + N-3) or we can add an independent clause "we skipped dinner." This gives us a supersentence --"Because we needed a good night's sleep after our strenuous afternoon running in the senior citizens' marathon, we skipped dinner."

Exercise 24

1. a) Joe dislikes cold weather, but he has recently taken up skiing.
   b) Although Joe dislikes cold weather, he has recently taken up skiing.
      (alternate version) Joe has recently taken up skiing, although he dislikes cold weather.

2. a) The two sisters who traveled to Europe stayed for six months.
   b) The two sisters traveled to Europe, and they stayed for six months.

3. a) These rosebushes will bloom for me or I'll give up gardening.
   b) (alternate version) Either these rosebushes will bloom for me or I'll give up gardening.

4. a) The camper who caused the forest fire had been unforgivably careless.
      The relative clause which modifies the subject must stand next to "camper."
   b) The camper, who had been unforgivably careless, caused the forest fire.

5. a) Because Howard's wife liked to swim, his family moved to the seacoast.
   b) Since Howard's wife liked to swim, his family moved to the seashore.
6. a) Most dogs like to paddle in the lake, but cats will never go into the water.
   b) Although most dogs like to paddle in the lake, cats will never go into the water.
7. The judge asked how long she had been driving.
8. a) If you plan to go to college, you should take high school more seriously.
   b) Because you plan to go to college, you should take high school more seriously.
9. The child wanted to know when I would read her a story.
10. We have all learned why the glaciers are melting.

CHAPTER 5

Exercise 25
1. No excuse for reckless driving is.
   Unusable unless we change "is" to "exists." However, no one would ever use that version.
   The use of "there" as a sentence opener serves the very useful purpose of putting an essential part of the sentence in the highlight position--the end of the sentence.
2. Several scholarship winners are among these high school graduates. Acceptable.
3. Sooner or later a time to pay your credit card bill comes.   Unusable unless we rewrite the sentence--Sooner or later a time to pay your credit card bill will come.
   Most people would prefer the "there" version because it puts the essential part of the sentence ("credit card bill") at the end
4. Music and dancing will be at our annual gala.
   Unusable. We must use "there." There will be music and dancing at our annual gala.
5. Only one solution for your problem seems to be.
   Unusable. We must use "there." There seems to be only one solution for your problem.

Exercise 26
1. "to" forms infinitive with "bark"
2. "to" forms infinitive with "clear away"
3. "to" is a preposition forming the prepositional phrase "to the two drivers"
4. a) "to" is a preposition forming the prepositional phrase "to our country house"

b) "to" forms infinitive with "start"
5. a) "to" forms infinitive with "understand"
   b) "to" forms infinitive with "listen"
   c) "to" is a preposition forming the prepositional phrase "to the professor's explanation"

Exercise 27
1. "who" --interrogator, pronoun subject of verb "is" (direct question)
2. "who"--relator, predicate pronoun after "are" (statement)
3. "who" --relator, pronoun subject of verb "left" (statement)
4. "which"--interrogator, adjective modifying noun "car" (direct question)
5. "which" --interrogator after an interrogative-forming verb ("wondered") in a statement containing an indirect question. "Which" also acts as an adjective modifying noun "restaurant."
6. "who"--interrogator, pronoun subject of verb "repair " (direct question) ("is going to" is an idiom meaning "will," which is a verb helper)
7. "where"--relator, adverb modifying "know" (statement)
8. "where"--interrogator following an interrogative-forming verb ("asked") in a statement containing an indirect question.
9. "why"--relator acting as an adverb modifying the verb "found out" in a statement.
10. "how"--relator in a statement. It is also an adverb modifying "qualify."

Exercise 28
1. subject of verb "tolls"--refers to "bell"
2. subject of verb "had"--refers to "bike"
3. place-holder subject of "is" so that the real subject--the infinitive phrase "to pay attention in a math class" --can be placed at the end of the sentence. This is a frequent practice when the subject is an infinitive phrase.
4. a) empty-word subject of verb "was" in a statement about time
   b) empty-word subject of verb "was" in a statement about weather
   This is an idiomatic use of "it."
5. a) empty-word subject of verb "was" in a statement about time.
   b) pronoun object of verb "found." It refers back to "snake."

Exercise 29
1. particle to intensify "clean"
2. preposition introducing the phrase "up the avenue"
3. particle to intensify "buckle"
4. adverb modifying verb "take"
5. particle with verb to mean "relinquish"

Exercise 30
1. demonstrative adjective modifying "car"

2. demonstrative pronoun (in partnership with "this")
3. subordinate conjunction (often dropped but understood)
4. referral pronoun (refers to previously mentioned noun cluster "your first summer at camp." Object of preposition "about"
5. relator--subject of verb "flooded" as well as clause connector

Exercise 31
1. "do"-- helper with "like" to form a yes/no question
2. "did"--helper with "not" to form negative
3 "does"--main verb in the sentence (meaning "performs")
4 "did"--replacement so that "worked" does not have to be repeated
5. "do"--helper with "not" to form negative
6. "do"--used for emphasis with "expect"
7. "do" –main verb meaning "perform"
8. "did"--helper with "not" to form negative
9. "did"--helper with "win" to ask direct question
10. "does"--helper with "start" to ask direct question

Exercise 32
1. The basketball team will not play some games this season.
                will not play some games this season, will it?
                won't play some games this season.
                won't play some games this season, will it?
2. The squad members were not ready to put out the fire.
                were not ready to put out the fire, were they?
                weren't ready to put out the fire.
                weren't ready to put out the fire, were they?
3. Our neighbors do not always park their car in their driveway.
              do not always park their car in their driveway, do they?
              don't always park their car in their driveway.
              don't always park their car in their driveway, do they?
4. Every passenger on the train was not reading a newspaper.
                    was not reading a newspaper, was he?
                    wasn't reading a newspaper.
                    wasn't reading a newspaper, was he?
Not every passenger on the train was reading a newspaper.
Not every passenger on the train was reading a newspaper, was he?
5. I do not know exactly what your score is.
   don't know exactly what your score is.
6. (To make this sentence negative, it is necessary to change "with" to "without.")
Without enough preparation, you will not be able to go to college.
                    you won't be able to go to college.
7. Aunt Rosa might not like maple syrup on her vanilla ice cream.
           mightn't like maple syrup on her vanilla ice cream.
(The tag "might she" is not American English.)

8. (This sentence is only possible in context--we assume that all the
   animals in the local zoo escaped.)
   Neither a goat nor an elephant ruined our front lawn.
   No goat or elephant ruined our front lawn.
9. Many people do not enjoy a cocktail before dinner.
              do not enjoy, a cocktail before dinner, do they?
              don't enjoy a cocktail before dinner.
              don't enjoy a cocktail before dinner, do they?
10. This hotel will not allow pets in your room.
               will not allow pets in your room, will it?
               won't allow pets in your room.
               won't allow pets in your room, will it?

Exercise 33
1. Had the basketball game ended in a tie?
   Hadn't the basketball game ended in a tie?
   The basketball game had ended in a tie, hadn't it?
2. Can her husband take time off from work?
   Can't her husband take time off from work?
   Her husband can take time off from work, can't he?
3. Did the charter fishing boat crash into the dock?
   Didn't the charter fishing boat crash into the dock?
   The charter fishing boat crashed into the dock, didn't it?
4. Should raw meat be kept in the refrigerator?
   Shouldn't raw meat be kept in the refrigerator?
   Raw meat should be kept in the refrigerator, shouldn't it?
5. Are the elephants waiting for their food?
   Aren't the elephants waiting for their food?
   The elephants are waiting for their food, aren't they?
6. Is the price of a first-night ticket too high?
   Isn't the price of a first-night ticket too high?
   The price of a first-night ticket is too high, isn't it?
7. Had the decision of the committee proved to be a mistake?
   Hadn't the decision of the committee proved to be a mistake?
   The decision of the committee had proved to be a mistake, hadn't it?
8. Without our help, might Ed's search for a job have ended in failure?
   Without our help, mightn't Ed's search for a job have ended in
   failure?
   Without our help, Ed's search for a job might have ended in failure,
   mightn't it?
   These are grammatically correct sentences, but they do not sound
   American. "Mightn't" seems vaguely British. It is more likely that
   Americans would choose to change the modal--
   Without our help, couldn't Ed's search for a job have ended in
   failure?

Without our help, Ed's search for a job could have ended in failure, couldn't it?
9. Did the builder file plans for a community hospital?
    Didn't the builder file plans for an emergency hospital?
    The builder filed plans for a community hospital, didn't he?
10. Was Tom conspicuous in a red plaid jacket?
    Wasn't Tom conspicuous in a red plaid jacket?
    Tom was conspicuous in a red plaid jacket, wasn't he?

Exercise 34
1. Who made his getaway at high noon?
2. How did he make his getaway?
3. When did he make his getaway?
4. Where had his confederate parked the getaway car?
5. Why did he use his confederate's car?
6. What did the confederate do to make the getaway possible?

Exercise 35
1. Alaska is part of the continental United States, isn't it?
2. Swimming with dolphins can be a thrilling experience, can't it?
3. The study of history will be enlightening, won't it?
4. Her gymnastic performance was not (wasn't) very impressive, was it?
5. Those tennis players are not (aren't) members of our country club, are they?

Exercise 36
1. How long will the intermission be?
2 .Where has your application been filed?
3. Why have the supplies run out?
4. When is the next train due?
5. Who is your boss?

Exercise 37
1. May I sit here?
    May I join you?
2. May I have a chair?
3. Will you move over, please?
    Would you kindly move over?
4. May I have this newspaper?
    Will you let me have this newspaper?
5. May I have a napkin?
    May I take one of these napkins?

Exercise 38
1. active (gave)
2. intransitive (neither active nor passive)
3. active (watch)
4. passive (was settled)
5. passive (is celebrated)
6. intransitive
7. passive (is considered)
8. active (inherited)
9. passive (was named)
10. passive (was presented)
11. passive (was determined)
12. passive (was administered)

Exercise 39
1. --
2. --
3. --
4. The Spanish settled America first.
5. We celebrate Thanksgiving as a family holiday. (When this sentence was made passive, the "by" phrase was dropped. The complete passive sentence would be "Thanksgiving is celebrated as a family holiday by us" or "by Americans" or "by everyone" or whatever would make sense.
6.--
7. We do not consider Election Day a holiday. (The "by" phrase was dropped.)
8.--
9. The board of directors named Elliott treasurer.
10. The governor presented this medal to me.
11. The police determined the cause of the accident almost at once. (The "by" phrase was dropped).
12. Medics administered first aid to the accident victim immediately. (The "by" phrase was dropped.).

CHAPTER 6

Exercise 40
1. noun cluster
2. prepositional phrase
3. adjective cluster
4. infinitive phrase
5. dependent clause (relative)
6. adverb cluster
7. pair (2 sentence patterns)
8. verbal adjective phrase

9. dependent clause (subordinate)
10. verb cluster
11. prepositional phrase
12. dependent clause (subordinate)
13. gerund phrase or noun cluster (depending on the context)
14. adjective cluster
15. dependent clause (relative)
16. verb cluster
17. prepositional phrase
18. noun cluster
19. series (verbal adjective phrases or gerund phrases)   (depending on
     the context.
20. adverb cluster

Exercise 41
1. in December—prepositional
2. the old freight depot—noun cluster
3. about instant approval—prepositional phrase
          instant approval—noun cluster
4. be willing to invest in new business—verb cluster
          to invest in new business—infinitive phrase
              in new business—prepositional phrase
              new business—noun cluster
5. provide care and compassion for needy adults--verb cluster
          care and compassion for needy adults—pair of nouns
                    for needy adults—prepositional
                                   phrase
                    needy adults—noun cluster

6.---
7. made the salad and made the cake—pair of verb clusters
          the salad—noun cluster
          the cake—noun cluster
8. by one of the suburban banks—prepositional phrase
        one of the suburban banks—noun (pronoun) cluster
          of the suburban banks—prepositional phrase
          the suburban banks—noun cluster
9. no one was able to put down a deposit—independent clause
        was able to put down a deposit—verb cluster
          able to put down a deposit—adjective cluster
            to put down a deposit—infinitive phrase
            put down a deposit—verb cluster
              a deposit—noun cluster
10. ready to leave with the rest of us—adjective cluster
      to leave with the rest of us—infinitive phrase
      leave with the rest of us—verb cluster
        with the rest of us—prepositional phrase

the rest of us—noun cluster

of us—prepositional phrase

11. spending part of the weekend at the movies--verbal adjective phrase or gerund phrase (depending on the context)

part of the weekend at the movies—noun cluster

of the weekend –prepositional phrase

the weekend—noun cluster

at the movies—prepositional phrase

the movies—noun cluster

(These are two separate prepositional phrases. One is not embedded in the other.)

12. they release the album too soon—independent clause

release the album too soon—verb cluster

the album—noun cluster

too soon—adverb cluster

13. ---

14. that he doesn't know the extent of his fortune--dependent clause (subordinate)

he doesn't know the extent of his fortune—independent clause

doesn't know the extent of his fortune—verb cluster

the extent of his fortune—noun cluster

of his fortune—prepositional phrase

his fortune—noun cluster

15. had invited for dinner—verb cluster

for dinner—prepositional phrase

16. to be crowded every Friday, Saturday, and Sunday—infinitive phrase

be crowded every Friday, Saturday, and Sunday --verb cluster

every Friday, Saturday, and Sunday—series of nouns

17. an almost impenetrable jungle—noun cluster

almost impenetrable—adjective cluster

18. full of crocodiles and mosquitoes—adjective cluster

of crocodiles and mosquitoes—prepositional phrase

crocodiles and mosquitoes—pair of nouns

19. on the sideboard—preposition

the sideboard—noun cluster

on the table—prepositional phrase

the table—noun cluster

on the couch—prepositional phrase

the couch—noun cluster

20. ---

CHAPTER 7

Exercise 42
1. fragment--no independent clause
    WHILE rain continued to-flood-streets
            N-1   VTr   N-3

    (AND) wind began to-bring-down-trees
            N-1   Vtr   N-3
    WHICH had increased to-gale-force
        N-1   Vintr
    This is a pair of clauses made dependent by the subordinate
    conjunction "while." The second dependent clause has an
    embedded dependent clause connected to it by the relator "which."
    Correction--add an independent clause--"While the rain continued
    to flood the streets and the wind, which had increased to gale force,
    began to bring down some of the old trees, we stayed indoors." (N-
    1 + Vintr) Note that the subordinate conjunction "while"
    subordinates both "the rain" and "the wind" clauses since they are a
    pair and hence operate as one unit.
2. correct sentence --one independent clause plus one dependent
    clause with embedded dependent clause..
    students talked
    N-1   Vintr
    WHILE lecturer picked up notes
            N-1   Vtr   N-3
    THAT he dropped (he dropped THAT)
            N-1 Vintr   N-3
3. correct sentence--one independent clause plus one dependent
    clause with embedded dependent clause.
    speaker   urged   supporters
    N-1   Vtr   N-3
    ALTHOUGH he knew (something)
            N-1 Vtr   N-3
    THAT Internet would play part
        N-1   Vtr   N-3
    Notice that the embedded "that" clause is the N-3 of the "although"
    clause.
4. run-on sentence--two independent clauses without a connector.
    town had days   children go
    N-1 Vtr N-3   N-1   Vintr
    Correction--separate them into two separate sentences: "Our town
    had too many snow days last winter" and "The children had to go to
    school until the day before the Fourth of July."
    Alternate correction--because of the obvious causal relationship
    between the two clauses, it would be logical to connect them with

the subordinate conjunction "because"--"Because our town had too many snow days last year, the children had to go to school until the day before the Fourth of July."

5. fragment--the independent clause has a subject "Tom" but no verb. The long preliminary verbal adjective phrase "Hoping..." has an embedded dependent clause --"that would set him on the path to medical school--" and "Tom" is modified by a dependent clause -- "who had previously worked in his father's shop on weekends"-- but these do not make up for the missing elements of the independent clause. We need to add a verb.

THAT set him
  N-1 Vtr N-3
Tom   --
  N-1 (no verb
WHO worked (modifies "Tom")
  N-1 Vintr

Correction--Add a verb to complete the main clause. "Hoping to win a college scholarship that would set him on the path to medical school, Tom, who had previously worked in his father's shop on weekends, quit in order to study." "Tom quit" (N-1 + Vintr). Although this would give us a grammatically correct sentence, it would be too overloaded to use. We need to split this supersentence into two statements-"Tom hoped to win a college scholarship that would set him on the path to medical school. Therefore he quit the weekend job in his father's shop in order to study." "Therefore" has no grammatical function.

6. correct sentence--one independent clause plus one dependent clause with an embedded dependent clause.
commuters find ways
   N-1   Vtr N-3
WHEN management decided (something)
         N-1   Vtr   N-3
THAT trains stop
     N-1 Vintr

The "that" clause is the N-3 of the "when" clause. (Reminder--negatives such as "not" and "never" have no grammatical significance.)

7. fragment--a dependent clause with an embedded dependent clause without any independent clause.
WHEN parents began taking...
     N-1   Vtr   N-3
WHICH offered
  N-1   Vintr

Correction--add an independent clause. "When parents began taking their children to the new town pool for swimming lessons which were offered free for the first six months, older taxpayers objected." (N-1 + Vintr).

8. correct sentence--an independent clause plus a dependent clause with an embedded dependent clause.

Jennie explained (something)
N-1   Vtr   N-3

THAT she won   prize
    N-1 Vtr   N-3

WHICH handed-down
   N-1   Vintr

The wordiness of the modifiers has no grammatical significance.

9. run-on sentence--two independent clauses, the second of which has an embedded dependent clause. There is no grammatical connector.

Working be experience
   N-1   Vlink   Nn-1

book   use   language
N-1   Vtr   N-3

THAT person understand (person understand THAT)
                        N-1   Vintr   N-3

Correction--the simplest solution would be to make two separate sentences--"Working with a computer can be an exhausting experience" and "The book of directions does not use language that the average person can understand."

However, since there is such an obvious causal relationship here, it would be logical to use the subordinate conjunction "because" and join the clauses into one supersentence. "Working with a new computer can be an exhausting experience because the book of directions does not use language that the average person can understand."

10. run-on sentence--two independent clauses. The first has an embedded dependent clause which, in turn, has an embedded dependent clause. The second independent clause has one dependent clause.

First independent clause--
detective realize (something)
N-1   Vtr   N-3

THAT most were   wind-surfers
    N-1 Vlink   Nn-1

WHO lived
  N-1   Vintr

Second independent clause--
they   provide   information
N-1   Vtr   N-3

ALTHOUGH they pretending to-be-ignorant
                N-1   Vtr   N-3

Correction--Separate the two independent clauses into two supersentences by putting a period after "wind-surfers" and capitalizing "they." " Nevertheless the detective did not realize that most of the youths who lived along the coast were excellent wind-surfers. They could provide useful information about tides and currents although they were pretending to be ignorant."

Exercise 43

1. run-on sentence--two independent clauses without a connector.

    hurricane forced ship   this created problem
    N-1   Vtr   N-3   N-1 Vtr   N-3
    Correction--separate the clauses into two sentences. "A hurricane forced the cruise ship scheduled to sail to South America to remain in its Florida port for three extra days. This created serious scheduling problems."

2. faulty parallelism--an independent clause connected to a prepositional phrase by a coordinate conjunction which requires a similar grammatical structure on each side.

    sport become popular
    N-1   Vlink   pred adj
            BUT
    with-older-people
    (not a clause)
    Correction--insert another prepositional phrase so that "but" is just connecting two prepositional phrases. "The strenuous sport of sky-diving has become very popular with-young-people BUT not-with-older-people." (The negator "not" has no grammatical importance.)

3. mis-subordination-- the more important idea has been expressed in a dependent clause instead of in the independent clause. Correction--shift the position of the subordinate conjunction "although" so that it introduces the other clause, thus making it dependent. "Although Tom and Walter bought a lottery ticket together, Walter was uneasy about gambling."

    ALTHOUGH Tom and Walter bought ticket
                 N-1 (pair)   Vtr   N-3
    Walter was uneasy
    N-1   Vlink pred adj

4. run-on sentence--two independent clauses without a connector. Although each has an embedded dependent clause, that does not make any difference.

    WHEN we arrived
         N-1 Vintr
    we took walk
    N-1 Vtr N-3

it   was   decision
N-1 Vlink   Nn-1
BECAUSE we   lost   way
            N-1 Vtr   N-3

Correction--make two sentences by ending the first statement after "dinner." "When we arrived at our hotel, we took a short walk before dinner. It was a bad decision because we lost our way."

5. mis-subordination--the more important statement is expressed in a dependent clause.

monkey   is named   Chippie
  N-1   Vlink   Nn-1
      WHO   snatched   sunglasses
      N-1   Vtr   N-3

Correction--use "who" to introduce the given independent clause. "A monkey, who is named Chippie, snatched the tourist's sunglasses." This will allow the left-over clause to be independent.

6. correct sentence

7. mis-subordination--the important information has been put into a dependent clause.

van was   model
N-1 Vlink   Nn-1
THAT ran-and-smashed window
  N-1 Vintr (a pair)   N-3

Correction--make "that" the introducer of the given independent clause. This will allow the left-over clause to be independent. "The van, that was a new GM model, ran up on the sidewalk and smashed a store window."

8. fragment--the independent clause has no verb. The two dependent clauses need a complete independent clause to connect to.

boys
N-1 ---
WHO came
  N-1 Vintr
WHICH they planned to-sell
(they planned to-sell-WHICH)
    N-1   Vtr   N-3

Correction--add a verb and a complement to the defective independent clause. "The young boys who came to the golf course every summer morning to search for lost balls which they planned to sell were very enterprising."

boys   were enterprising
N-1   Vlink   pred adj
     WHO came
     N-1 Vintr
WHICH they planned to-sell (they planned to-sell-WHICH)
                          N-1 Vtr   N-3

9. faulty parallelism--the coordinate conjunction "and" is connecting one independent clause and one dependent clause. A coordinate conjunction must connect two grammatically equal items.
   member opposed tax
   N-1   Vtr   N-3
   and
   THAT it solve problem
      N-1 Vtr   N-3
   Correction--delete "and" and substitute "because" for "that. "The council member opposed the new tax because it would not solve the budget problem."
10. fragment--the independent clause has a subject but no verb.
    children
        N-1   ---
    WHO took bus
      N-1 Vtr N-3
    Correction--add a verb and complement to the defective independent clause--"The children, who took a bus to the summer day camp located on a lake about ten miles from their town, were a happy group."
    children were   group
      N-1   Vlink   Nn-1

CHAPTER 8

Exercise 44
a)
1. silently--adverb modifying "waited"
2. in the packed gymnasium--prepositional phrase modifying "waited"
3. flushed and weary young people--noun cluster, appositive (renaming) of "the contestants."
4. to hear the judge announce the winner--infinitive phrase modifying "waited"
5. waiting silently--verbal adjective phrase modifying "contestants"
6. as if they had abandoned all hope of winning--subordinate clause modifying "waited"
7. with high hopes--prepositional phrase modifying "waited"
8. in the packed gymnasium--prepositional phrase modifying "waited" seated before the judges--verbal adjective phrase modifying "contestants"
9. sitting silently and smiling nervously--a pair of verbal adjective phrases modifying "contestants"
10. to hear the judges announce the decision and to find out what the winning point score was--a pair of infinitive phrases modifying "waited"

11. silently, nervously, expectantly--a series of adverbs modifying
    "waited"
12. In the packed gymnasium, across from the judges, directly below a
    cluster of flags--a series of three prepositional phrases modifying
    "waited" Directly is an adverb modifying "below." It does not affect
    the grammatical balance of the series.
13. Heads up, faces tense, eyes bright--a series of noun clusters
    modifying "contestants"
14. silently--adverb modifying "waited'
    eyes bright with excitement—noun cluster modifying "contestants"--
    This is actually the object of an dropped preposition "with," forming
    a prepositional phrase.
    This was a stylistic choice to avoid the repetition of "with."
    Since language rules are not as rigid as math rules, an experienced
    writer can take occasional liberties.
15. while they waited to hear the name of the winner--subordinate
    clause modifying "sat"

b)
All the sentences containing the word "silently" are too wordy because
it can be taken for granted that contestants wait silently for a decision.
If they are noisy, that would be worth mentioning.
 Sentence 12 is too long because of the unnecessary details "across
from the judges" and "directly below a cluster of flags." These details
weaken the drama of the sentence.
Sentence 6 is overwritten. "As if they had abandoned all hope of
winning" is too extreme to be believable.
Sentence 15 is anti-climactic. After the long introductory clause, the
reader expects something more than "the contestants sat silently."
Sentence 2 is effective and sentence 13 would be effective if "silently"
were to be dropped. Sentence 3 would be effective without "young
people." This unnecessary detail takes away from the vivid "flushed
and weary."
Whether or not the individual student agrees with these criticisms is
unimportant. What is important is that the student sees that sentences
can be made more effective by a careful choice of details and the
exercise of caution about wordiness.

Exercise 45
1. an attractive group of young people waiting to hear the decision--a
   noun cluster that gives more information about the subject noun
   "contestants." This second noun or noun cluster, an appositive, is
   generally short. Since this one is fairly long, it is placed at the end
   of the sentence. This keeps the predicate adjective "silent"--the
   most meaningful word in the sentence--from being overlooked by
   the reader.

2. on the sidelines & in the packed gymnasium-- two prepositional phrases modifying "sat." It is the normal position for modifiers of the verb when there is no complement. These two phrases are not a pair; they work independently of each other.

3. normal verb + object

4. slimmed by exercise, disciplined by practice, bright-eyed with anticipation—a series of verbal adjective phrases modifying "figures," the predicate noun (Nn-1). Since the phrases are identical in construction (verbal adjective + prepositional phrase), they give the sentence a satisfying little flourish at the end like a three-note chord in music.

5. waiting to hear the decision, verbal adjective phrase modifying "contestants." The position of this phrase next to "coaches" creates some doubt as to whether it is just the coaches who are waiting or both groups that are waiting. Putting the phrase at the beginning of the sentence would attach it to "contestants"—waiting to hear the decision, the contestants. However, this shifts the weight of the sentence too heavily into the subject area with a verbal phrase modifier to the left of the noun and another verbal modifier (adjective dependent clause) to the right of the noun. The simplest way to eliminate the original ambiguity and to avoid the frontal shift is to add a dash and the word "all" after "coaches." This gives us "The contestants, who had been training for months, sat with their coaches—all waiting to hear the decision."

6. expectantly-- an adverb modifying "waited"
   for the decision--prepositional phrase modifying the verb. Both are normal followers of the verb.

7.expectantly,-- adverb modifying "gazed"
   at the judges-- prepositional phrase modifying "gazed"
   Without a complement, a sentence frequently ends with trailing verb modifiers.

8. for the judges to announce the decision--an infinitive phrase introduced by "for." "The judges" is the subject of the verb "announce" within the phrase. The whole phrase modifies the main verb "waited" and is in the normal position for an adverb modifier.

9. not only to hear the decision—
   but also to demonstrate to the spectators that they were disciplined athletes-- a pair of infinitive phrases modifying the adjective "silent." This is an unusual sentence because "sat" is working as a linking verb (in place of "were") taking a predicate adjective "silent." The sentence could just as well have been "The contestants were silent..." but the writer may have wanted to strike a little note of alliteration with the two words each beginning with "s."
   (Alliteration--when two or three adjacent words each begin with the same letter. This is a device rooted in the original form of the English language—Anglo-Saxon.)

10. as if ready for anything
   as if all their training had not been leading up to this moment—
   a pair of subordinate clauses modifying the verb "sat." The first of
   the two clauses has been shortened from "as if they were ready for
   anything." Only an experienced writer should attempt this. The
   intent here was to state the bare fact first and then to gain further
   emphasis by replacing the generalization with a specific statement.
   Some of these sentences might strike a reader as unnecessarily
   complicated, as if the writer tried to give the subject matter too
   much importance..

Exercise 46

1. --
2. silent and tense-- a pair of adjectives modifying "figures." This is
   the normal position for a noun modifier consisting of more than one
   word.
3. tense but cheerful-- a pair of adjectives modifying "contestants." This
   is the same kind of post-noun modifier we have in sentence #2.
4. --
5. who had been training for months-- dependent clause modifying
   "contestants." Since it is more than a single-word adjective, it must
   follow the noun.
6. their eyes fixed on the judges-- a verbal adjective phrase in which
   the verbal adjective "fixed" has its own subject "gaze." This is the
   normal post-noun modifier position.
7. waiting for the decision-- a verbal adjective phrase modifying
   "contestants." It is in the normal post-noun position.
8. in the aftermath of their precise and beautiful routines-- a
   prepositional phrase modifying "waited." While this is grammatically
   correct, it risks losing the reader because of the long wait for the
   main verb "waited." It would be more effective placed at the
   beginning of the sentence. In the aftermath of their precise and
   beautiful routines, the contestants waited for the judges to
   announce the decision.
9. --
10. --

Exercise 47

1. "The strain of continuing success in a competitive field" is the N-3 in
   this sentence pattern, but it has been put first for emphasis. The
   basic pattern is N-1 + vtrans + N-3 ("he knew strain"). This reversal
   is effective.
2. "Less changeable than a garden of mixed flowers" is the predicate
   adjective in the sentence pattern N-1 Vbe + predicate adj (expanse
   is changeable). Putting the predicate adjective first in this sentence
   makes it less effective than it would be in normal word order

because the reader does not find out what is being talked about until he comes to the second half of the sentence. The normal word order is "An expanse of lawn bordered by evergreen shrubs is less changeable than a garden of mixed flowers."

3. Again we have the predicate adjective put into the subject position. The sentence pattern is N-1 + Vbe + pred adj ("he was hard"). The reversal is effective.

4. This is another case of reversal where the predicate adjective has been put in the subject position. The sentence pattern is N-1 + Vbe + pred adj ("people are fortunate"). This reversal is desirable because the subject is complicated. The reader has to hold too much meaning in mind before he finds out the most important word in the sentence, the predicate adjective "fortunate."

5. The postponement of the subject ("the new star") in this sentence is awkward. The opening construction, an adjective cluster ("sure to be signed again by the film producer") is long and not very important in terms of meaning. It should follow the noun it modifies ("star") in normal fashion so that the reader is not distracted from the meaningful part of the sentence "besieged by the press." ("The new star, sure to be signed again by the film producer, was besieged by the press" is the better word order.)

Exercise 48
1. Four main verbs--four sentence patterns:
   (Note--the term "main verb" is used to indicate the essential verb in a sentence pattern. It is not a helper, nor is it a weak verb form like a verbal noun (gerund), a verbal adjective (participle), or an infinitive.
   A sentence pattern can form an independent clause or a dependent clause. If it is introduced by a subordinating connector, it is a dependent clause.)
   a) guide decided (something)--independent clause
   b) we would continue our climb to the summit--dependent clause connected by "that"
   c) weather remained favorable--dependent clause connected by "as"
   d) where we remain overnight--dependent clause connected by "where"
   (Although this sentence looks complicated on the page, its structure is not unusual.)
2. Three main verbs--three sentence patterns:
   a) Tom and nephew going...
   b) he decided to stay ...
      (These are independent clauses joined by the coordinate conjunction ":but.")
   c) when boy received game--dependent clause introduced by "when"

(The supersentence, though long, is not unnecessarily complicated. However, there should not be too many of these in a single paragraph.)

3. Five main verbs--five sentence patterns:
   a) when comedian went backstage--dependent clause connected by "when"
   (Remember that the connector always appears at the beginning of the dependent clause.)
   b) show ended--dependent clause connected by "after"
   c) he found dressing room --independent clause
   d) who wanted autograph--dependent clause connected by "who"
   e) he become famous--dependent clause connected by "because"
   (While this supersentence is not ungrammatical, it is clumsy. There are too many details, in the form of dependent clauses, packed into it.)
4. Four main verbs--four sentence patterns
   a) boat chugged...--independent clause
   b) which we boarded...-- dependent clause connected by "which"
   c) we reached...village--dependent clause connected by "until"
   d) where we went ashore--dependent clause connected by "where"
   (This supersentence is acceptable, but it would have been easier to read if the final clause had been made into a simple sentence to follow the long one--"There we went ashore for an early lunch.")
5. Five main verbs--five sentence patterns
   a) he know...-- dependent clause connected by "since"
   b) who assigned..-- dependent clause connected by "who"
   c) where city hall was located--dependent clause connected by "where"
   d) he telephoned secretary--independent clause
   e) whom he met..--dependent clause connected by "whom"
   (This is another clumsy sentence with too many dependent clauses. The final detail--"whom he had met a few days before"--is irrelevant to the sentence message.)
6. Four main verbs—four sentence patterns
   a) radio was invented--dependent clause connected by "before"
   b) people be late..-- independent clause
   c) who had ...clocks--dependent clause connected by "who"
   d) they forgot to wind--dependent clause connected by "if"
   (This sentence is acceptable. Four connected sentence patterns generally make for an acceptable sentence if the details in the dependent clauses are relevant to the basic sentence message. Five or more connected clauses generally produce a clumsy supersentence.)
7. Four main verbs--four sentence patterns
   a) it was autumn--independent clause
   b) weatherman predicted snowstorm--independent clause

(These two clauses are connected by the coordinate conjunction "and.")

c) that block ...roads-- dependent clause connected by "that"

d) family ...planned to drive..-- independent clause joined by coordinate conjunction "but"

(This is a grammatically correct supersentence but it is stylistically inadvisable because it is overloaded.)

8. Four main verbs--four sentence patterns

   a) William expected to get...-- independent clause

   b) company lost contract-- dependent clause connected by "unless"

   c) that was coming up-- dependent clause connected by "that"

   d) holidays began-- dependent clause connected by "before"

   (This is an acceptable sentence but the message would be more effective if expressed in two sentences rather than in one.)

9. Six main verbs--six sentence patterns

   a) bills increasing..--dependent clause connected by "because"

   b) he said (something)--independent clause

   c) they move...--dependent clause connected by "that"

   d) which help them (to) stay..-- dependent clause connected by "which"

   e) they worked out..--dependent clause connected by "that"

   f) when son needed money..-- dependent clause connected by "when"

   (This is an overloaded sentence with too many details.)

10. Three main verbs--three sentence patterns

    a) Nancy took children...--dependent clause connected by "whenever"...

    b) she take (something)--independent clause

    c) she juggled..(something)--dependent clause connected by "while"

    (While this supersentence contains an unusual number of details, it is acceptable because the overloading of the sentence is intended to give the reader the same sensation that Nancy has--too much to handle all at once. This stylistic device is only for a skillful writer who knows when this kind of overloading will be effective.)

INDEX

194